"I share a deep affinity with the Popcaks and the way they present the Faith. Their latest book, *Just Married*, is loaded with their typical winsome wisdom and advice. They help newly married couples unpack the great mystery of marriage and discover the divine love story that is behind their own. Every married couple—newly married or otherwise—will benefit from this book."

Christopher West
Author of *Fill These Hearts*

"*Just Married* should be required reading for every recently married Catholic Couple. Christian marriage is a call to heroic love. It should not be surprising that living this vocation well does not happen without prayer and effort. Greg and Lisa provide many helpful insights into the challenges that young couples encounter as well as practical strategies on how to overcome what otherwise will become obstacles to their happiness. Married couples honor and praise God most beautifully by striving daily to grow in their love for each other in the Lord. There is nothing more important that a couple can do to build up the Church and make a better world than to do whatever it takes to make their marriage strong and healthy. The Popcaks provide a practical pathway to help couples enjoy the abundant life God desires for them in this world and to help each other make it together to heaven."

Archbishop Joseph F. Naumann
Archdiocese of Kansas City in Kansas

"Thank you, Greg and Lisa! *Just Married* is a treasure for today's newly (and not so newly!) married couples. A guide this rich with grace and wisdom can only come from a deeply faithful Catholic married couple seasoned through years of marriage, professional practice, and prayer. This is theology of the body for the newly married couple."

Damon Owens
Executive Director
Theology of the Body Institute

"We are so happy to be able to give the young people in our lives a copy of *Just Married*. This is a book filled with personal testimony, evidence from science, years of counseling experience, and, most importantly, a hopeful vision of marriage rooted in faith and nourished by prayer."

Tim and Sue Muldoon
Authors of *Six Sacred Rules for Families*

JUST MARRIED

The Catholic Guide
to Surviving and Thriving in the
First Five Years of
Marriage

Dr. Greg and Lisa Popcak
Authors of *Parenting with Grace*

AVE MARIA PRESS AVE Notre Dame, Indiana

Excerpt from *For Better . . . Forever!: A Catholic Guide to Lifelong Marriage* (2nd ed.) by Gregory K. Popcak, copyright 2009 by Our Sunday Visitor, Huntington, IN, 46750. Used with permission of the publisher.

Founded in 1865, Ave Maria Press is a ministry of the United States Province of Holy Cross.

www.avemariapress.com

Paperback: ISBN-10 1-59471-280-8, ISBN-13 978-1-59471-280-7

E-book: ISBN-10 1-59471-281-6, ISBN-13 978-1-59471-281-4

Cover image © thinkstockphotos.com

Cover and text design by Katherine Robinson.

Printed and bound in the United States of America.

Library of Congress Cataloging-in-Publication Data is available.

Contents

Do You Have What It Takes?

The first five years of marriage can be a roller coaster. The feelings of love, romance, and joy can be so intense as you are starting your life together, but so can those feelings of anxiety, insecurity, and anger. Despite how long you and your spouse have known each other, marriage can change everything—for better and for worse. With marriage comes a new level of commitment, a challenge to cultivate a deeper level of trust. You can't help surrendering more of yourselves to each other, and that can be a wonderful thing, but it also raises the stakes—and the potential challenges—a couple can face.

The majority of divorces (about 20 percent) occur within the first ten years of marriage with about 10 percent occurring in the first five years and another 10 percent occurring in the second five years of marriage.[1] That's not surprising since the early years of marriage represent the time that couples are getting to know each other on a whole different level. The good news is that you can use the early years of your marriage to establish truly important healthy-relationship habits that can strengthen your bond today and keep your marriage growing stronger every day for as long as you both shall live.

The first five years of marriage represent the time that a couple is laying the foundation for a sound relationship. The habits and attitudes you cultivate now can spell the difference between a marriage that is built on sand and a marriage that can grow more passionate and beautiful, not just in spite of the toughest tests life can throw at it, but also because of the way you have braved those challenges together. Your marriage can be a great love story that your children tell their children—a story that inspires everyone you know because of your example.

In order for your marriage to become that great love story there are certain things you need to establish in your early years together because relationships tend to build and grow on precedent. The way you live now can predict the attitudes you will have toward your marriage ten, twenty, thirty years from now. Although the challenges life throws at you will change, the patterns you lay down now will predict how easy it will be for the two of you to overcome those challenges while still having time and energy for each other. The couple that takes these early years for granted and assumes that you will always have the same kind of time that you have for each other once kids and careers start kicking into high gear will be in for a huge and unpleasant surprise. By contrast, the couple that is intentional about laying down good marriage habits in the first five years has a much greater likelihood of staying close, strong, and happy when life starts picking up speed.

Do You Have What It Takes?

Almost every newly married couple we encounter has two things in common. First, they are deeply in love with each other and rightly excited about the lives they are building together. They are passionate about each other, and hopeful about a bright future filled with blessings. But second, underneath that mutual love, joy, and hope, almost every newly married couple is also a little terrified. They wonder if they have what it takes to make it "until death do us part." Almost every couple we talk to in our years of marriage ministry ask us one basic question; "How can we know if we have what it takes to make it to 'happily ever after'?"

We can give you the answer to that question right now. Do you have what it takes? *Yes!* Absolutely, you have what it takes to have a great Catholic marriage. Contrary to what you might have heard elsewhere, it doesn't matter where you've come from, what your background is, or what your family of origin did or did not give you. We know from years of marriage research that what separates so-called "marriage masters" from "marriage disasters" is not magic or history; it's a set of teachable skills that happy couples have either picked up along the way or are willing to learn "on the job," as it were.[2] Throughout this book, we'll explore the things you need to do now, in the early years of your life together, that will help you create the marriage God wants you to have, a marriage founded on the kind of love that satisfies your soul and makes the world stand up and take notice of what God can do when a couple lets him into their home.

While there are many good habits you can cultivate to lay the foundation for a great Catholic marriage, ultimately it is your willingness to have an unwavering commitment to four things that will help you and your spouse become "marriage masters":

1. individual and couple prayer

2. nurture your love

3. each other, but an even stronger commitment to your vows

4. learn new skills when new challenges come instead of giving into a tendency to blame your marriage or spouse for being "broken"

Each of these is rooted in solid research that examines what separates marriage success stories from marriage nightmares, and each of these is borne out in our experience—of which we will share a bit with you in this chapter. Let's look at each of these four commitments.

Individual and Couple Prayer

Couples who pray together stay together. Research consistently shows that couples who share and cultivate their religious commitment (both at church *and* at home) are significantly more likely to be happy together and stay together for a lifetime.[3]

The early years of marriage are the best time to establish those regular rituals of couple prayer time, faithful Mass attendance, and regular confession that give you the grace you need to be patient and loving with each other as you confront each other's weaknesses head-on.

You need to be absolutely committed to your prayer life and be willing to let God teach you how to love each other with his love. Your human love will simply dry up on some days. It can't be helped. Marriage is hard work, and people inevitably burn out from hard work. Every couple goes through it periodically over the lifetime of their marriage. You don't have to be afraid of this happening (although, admittedly, it's never a pleasant experience at the time), but on those days when you feel your own ability to love running dry, you need to have something to lean on to jump-start your heart and start loving each other again. Your own experience of God's love via your commitment to an active and constant prayer life is the most reliable way to restart your loving actions (and the loving feelings which follow those actions). Ecclesiastes 4:12 says, "Where a lone man may be overcome, two together can resist. A three-ply cord is not easily broken." In other words, you might not have the strength to create a great marriage on your own, but if both of you are committed to leaning on God (the third braid in the "three-ply cord" of Christian marriage), you will be unbreakable no matter what weight life asks you to carry.

For reasons we'll get into shortly, God truly does want you to have a fantastic marriage. If you give him the opportunity through couple prayer, he will teach you everything you need to know about creating a passionate, fulfilling, joyful, lifelong love. True, he won't send you an instruction manual, but he'll do something better: he will open up new depth of your hearts to each other in ways you never dreamed possible and empower you to experience a love you never even knew was possible to receive—much less give. We'll walk you through the steps of couple prayer later on, but for now, start wrapping your head around the idea that praying together has real power to make a tough marriage terrific and a good marriage great.

Nurture Your Love

Truly successful couples know that love doesn't just happen. You have to be committed to building the fire on an ongoing basis. When we built our home, we were unsure about having a fireplace. We couldn't really afford it, but by making adjustments in other places, we were able to scrape together enough money to make it possible. Years later, we've been so glad we made room for that expense. It adds so much romance and charm to our home. One of our favorite things to do in the cooler months is to build a big fire and spend time reading and playing board games together in front of the hearth. Sometimes we break for high tea in front of the fire with little finger sandwiches and tasty pastries that we've baked or purchased from our favorite pastry shop. And after the kids go to bed, cuddling by the fire is a great way to spend a romantic evening at home.

But keeping that fire going takes real effort. It means chopping, splitting, and stacking wood in the spring so it has time to cure for the following fall. It means carrying wood from the outdoor woodpile to the indoor rack so it's handy when we need it. When the fire is built, it means stirring the coals on a regular basis to get the hottest embers at the bottom of the pile back to the top and adding more logs every few hours so that the flames don't run out of fuel. That's the part they don't show in movies. There's real work that goes on behind the scenes that keeps the flames burning hot.

The same is true for love. Smart couples understand that to keep the fires of their love burning strong, they need to tend the flame by doing those little, extraordinary things for each other. Little surprises such as love notes in a lunch bag; calls to say, "I was thinking of you"; bringing home your spouse's favorite ice cream instead of yours; doing that chore your spouse hates so that you can say, "I want to make your life easier and more pleasant"; ordering and wearing that new lingerie on a night when you might rather just pass out because you want to say, "I still want you"; and many other little, thoughtful gestures go a long way to stirring the coals and keeping the embers of your love burning hot.

Too many couples think that the fires of love kindle themselves and that somehow the wood carries itself to the hearth while they just lie around on a bearskin rug, basking in the warmth. Real love—even real romantic love—doesn't work that way. Later on, we'll share some surefire ways to keep your hearts warm and your passion burning bright throughout your years together. But for now it is important to remember that loving feelings follow loving actions. If the fire looks like it's getting a little low, don't panic, and for heaven's sake, don't whine about it. Go get some more wood! Stir the embers. Don't wait for your mate to do the work. Inspire your partner by taking the first steps and do something loving. Your mutual commitment to tending the flames of your friendship and passion by doing little, loving things for each other every day—no matter how busy, tired, sick, or frustrated you might feel in the moment—is one of the things that will help make your marriage be a welcome, safe, and happy place even when the storms of life are blowing hard against your home.

It is important to remember that loving feelings follow loving actions.

As you'll see in a bit, we've been through a lot in our years together, and life got really hard pretty quickly in those first months and years after we said "I do." When we reviewed some of these early-marriage experiences we're about to share with you, we looked at each other and said, "Holy cow! We really went through a lot in those first few years together!" The reason it came as such a surprise to us, though, was that no matter how hard or scary life became, we always worked hard to take care of each other. Even when we were tired, stressed, scared, and sure that the universe was going to fall down on top of us, we worked hard to remember to make that call to say, "I love you," to say that prayer together, to do that dreaded chore for the other, to give that thoughtful or silly gift that would bring a smile to the other's face, to write that note that said we couldn't stop thinking about each other even when we were apart, to make time for affection and lovemaking—especially when we were tired or stressed—and to do a million other little things that made our marriage a safe shelter from the storm.

Because of that genuine, sustained effort to keep feeding the flames of love, when we look back, we don't really connect with how terrifying it all really was and how stupid we really were. We look back and see some of the best times in our lives together.

People say that love is a mystery. But it isn't love that's a mystery. The mystery is how such simple things as the ones we mentioned above can make even the hardest day feel as a gift when you are standing next to the person God gave you to be his best blessing in your life.

Commitment to Your Vows
(Even More Than to Each Other)

In addition to tending the fires of your love, you need to make an unwavering commitment to your marriage vows. In the early years of marriage, especially if you've been arguing more than you expected—and any couples do—it can be very tempting to begin wondering if you didn't make a mistake and if it wouldn't be easier to cut your losses sooner than later. No matter how wonderful the person you married is, you may have already experienced days when you look at your spouse and think to yourself, "What was I thinking?"

The key to making it through these days—both now and throughout the rest of your married life—is making

a commitment, not just to each other, but also to the
marriage itself. This means making a commitment to
your vows. Research by the Relationship Institute at
UCLA shows that while almost every couple is committed to each other, those couples who make an additional
commitment to the relationship itself—vowing to work
on the marriage even when it isn't fun and they don't
feel that great about their spouse—have much greater
chances to have marriages that are happy and last a
lifetime.[4]

Even when staying committed to your marriage
doesn't make emotional sense, your long-term success,
not to mention your personal integrity, depends on
your ability to keep the marital promises you made to
God and yourself even when you feel as if your spouse
doesn't deserve your commitment. No one gets married with the intention of getting divorced. The breakup
of a marriage isn't only devastating for the loss of the
relationship. It is also devastating to a person's sense
of self. Feeling like a failure, wondering what is wrong
with you, and wondering if you will even find happiness are all terrible things to have to struggle with.
There is a Facebook meme that shows an image of an
old couple with the caption, "When asked how they
stayed together for sixty-five years, the couple replied,
'We come from a time where if something is broken you
fix it, not throw it away.'" There is real truth behind this
sentiment.

The thought that there will be days when the only
thing that keeps you hanging in there is your commitment to the marriage itself doesn't have to scare
you. Every couple experiences this at least briefly,

but certainly periodically, throughout a marriage. But remember, these times pass and the loving times come back—often stronger than ever. And couples who pray together, tend the fires of their love, maintain their commitment to their vows, and do all the other things we describe in this book bounce back much faster and more happily than couples who are less intentional about their marriage. Since you are now "in the know" you have nothing to fear.

Skill Building over Blaming

Finally, you need an ongoing, unwavering commitment to always be willing to learn new skills to overcome new challenges. According to SmartMarriages, an organization of marriage experts dedicated to promoting research that supports healthy marriages, successful marriages depend on skill, not your family of origin (smartmarriages.com). No newly married couple knows what they are doing when it comes to marriage. No one. Not even the people who came from the best families of origin on the planet. In fact, the more you think you have marital success figured out, the more likely it is that you will be in for a rude surprise. After all, it's one thing to watch Mom and Dad do it well. It's another thing to do it yourself. And if you didn't come from an ideal background (and who does?), this is even more true. When you hit hard times and begin feeling the urge to turn against each other (or when you all too willingly give in to that urge from time to time), you must remember that it is not because your marriage is flawed. It is simply because you don't know what you are doing and you need new skills. We want you to remember four little words that will help you get through these times. Ready?

NEVER BLAME YOUR MARRIAGE

Write it down. Tattoo it on the back of your hand. Memorize it. Chant it. Say it until you can dance to it. Marriages do not have lives of their own. A marriage only has the life a husband and wife give it. People say things such as, "*It* just didn't work." or "*It* just didn't make sense anymore." "*It* just died." Remember this. There is no *it*. There is just you, your spouse, and God. If your marriage is dying on the vine, it isn't because *it* (your marriage) is broken. It is simply that you don't currently have the skills to nurture it under the pressures you are currently facing. Get those skills. Read good self-help books; go on a marriage retreat; join a support group; get therapy. Resources for all of these options are listed in the back of this book. The good news is that research consistently shows that couples

> No marriage ever failed because a couple lacked skills. Rather, marriages fail because couples are too prideful to admit that they need to acquire new skills.

who have the "don't blame the marriage" attitude and, instead, commit to acquiring skills when they hit hard times have much higher levels of marital satisfaction and longevity.[5] No marriage ever failed because a couple lacked skills. Rather, marriages fail because couples are too prideful to admit that they need to acquire new skills. As it says in Proverbs 11:2, "When pride comes, disgrace follows. But with the humble is wisdom."

The above represent the four commitments you need to make to have a great, Catholic marriage. Because anyone can choose to make these four commitments, we are confident that you do indeed have what it takes to create a joyful marriage that can stand the test of time.

Just to prove that anyone can have a great marriage, let us share a little of our story.

⌾UR STORY

We met as students in our junior year at university, and we had what was, by any account, a whirlwind courtship. We both had very active individual prayer lives, and we quickly began praying with each other in small ways (going to Mass together, asking for God's blessing on our relationship, saying grace before meals, taking small prayer times together, etc.). Through this process, we both felt strongly that God was calling us together. We both knew right from the beginning that the love we had for each other really came from God's own heart.

It wasn't just that we were attracted to each other and liked doing many of the same things; we also connected deeply with regard to our values, beliefs, and the goals for our lives—probably not unlike you and your spouse. Even so, through our prayer life together, God made it abundantly clear that something very powerful and unique was happening in our relationship. For that reason, even though we weren't officially engaged, on the anniversary of our first month of dating, we reserved the university chapel for the day after our graduation the following year "just in case" things worked out as we thought they would.

We became engaged on the anniversary of our second month together. This was not our plan. Greg wanted to wait at least until we got back from summer break to propose. We both realized things were moving weirdly, though wonderfully, fast—emotionally and spiritually speaking. On the one hand, we were so excited about what God was doing in our lives; on the other hand, we heard our parents' and friends' voices screaming, "What's the hurry? Don't rush into things! Be reasonable!"

> **Greg says:** Even though my heart wanted to rush ahead, I wanted to at least try to appear to be sane about it, and I knew that it would be completely insane to get engaged after only two months together. Besides, I had a whole romantic plan in my head of how I wanted to ask Lisa to marry me.
>
> Every year, my parents and I took a trip to Niagara Falls. I planned to invite her to come with us. I'd have the ring. We would have dinner at a romantic restaurant overlooking the falls. After dinner, as we walked in the mist from the Niagara River and as the fireworks shot overhead, I would ask her to marry me. My family would be there to make her feel welcome. It would be perfect.
>
> Instead, I took a less glamorous approach. On a trip to the grocery store with Lisa at the end of the spring semester, we got to talking in the parking lot about life, the universe,

and everything, and it all just made sense—
or rather, "we" just made sense. I wasn't sure
what possessed me at the time—although I do
believe it was the Holy Spirit now—but all of a
sudden I couldn't hold back anymore. It wasn't
just attraction. It wasn't just that I happened to
enjoy spending time with her. It was something
deeper.

In his spiritual exercises, St. Ignatius of
Loyola described three ways of knowing what
God wants for you; the first and most perfect
way of knowing is "Clarity beyond Doubt." The
great spiritual director Fr. Timothy Gallagher
describes this kind of knowing God's will as
an overwhelming sense that God has already
made the decision for you. All you have to do
is get out of his way by saying, "Yes." I haven't
had many experiences like that in my life, but
this was one of them that I have never doubted.
In that most unlikely and unplanned moment, I
surprised myself by blurting out, "Lisa Morgan,
will you marry me?"

Lisa says: I think I surprised him even more
by saying, "Yes!" I had no idea that Greg was
going to propose, but I just knew I had to say
yes despite knowing it was completely crazy.
Like him, I just felt the incredible rightness of
it all—as if God was urging me to say yes and
putting all of his weight behind my answer. I
just had to get out of God's way. It didn't matter

that Greg didn't have a ring. I knew in my soul it was right.

But then Greg did something strange (well, stranger). He told me he'd be right back, and he jumped out of the car and ran into the store! I didn't know what he was doing. I thought maybe he changed his mind the second I answered him! All I could do was wait. And while I waited, I was terrified. I just kept thinking, "What did I do? Why did I say yes? I know it's right, but this is crazy!"

It turns out that he felt so awkward proposing without a ring that he decided to buy me roses on the spot. He was in and out of the store in record time with a dozen beautiful red roses, which added the perfect touch to our special (and however odd) engagement.

In hindsight, the craziness and lack of preparedness of our proposal was really a foreshadowing of what was to come. Not only did we not have a ring, we didn't have college degrees, jobs, a house, or any kind of plan for the future.

Greg says: We did wait until after our senior year—the day after graduation—to get married. And what a year that was. All of our friends treated us as if we were nuts. Our families weren't sure what to think, although Lisa's family was much more supportive than mine. My mother took it especially hard and was really mercilessly angry at me the entire year leading up to the wedding. My dad didn't know what to think. I don't really blame them, since we must have appeared completely insane. But it was a tough year with almost no support and a whole lot of antagonism on top of that. I don't really think anyone was truly happy for us. For me, except for the excitement I felt about our future and the deep, spiritual sense that sticking with it was unquestionably the right thing to do, it was one of the most miserable engagements a man could experience, especially since we were separated both for the summer and our second semester senior year. (Lisa graduated a semester before me and went back home to work for a few months before the wedding to try to save some money, especially since I was planning to go to grad school after graduation.) I was lonely, alone, and almost constantly antagonized by both family and friends about our engagement. It was a tough way to start planning a life with someone.

Lisa says: Greg says my family was more supportive. I guess that's true in the sense that they didn't argue with me about getting married. But when it came time to get ready for the wedding, even though she could certainly afford to do more, my mom refused to give us more than about one thousand dollars for the ceremony, since we were having it at school and so few of my family or her friends would be willing to make the trip. She didn't really understand my faith or why we would want to be married in the Church. (She had completely, and angrily, rejected the Catholic faith of her childhood. I came back to the Church as a teenager.) She just kept suggesting that we should elope and she'd give us the little bit of money she would have spent on the wedding to start our lives together. I felt totally unsupported by my mom, as if the wedding was about her and her wishes, not mine. If we weren't going to do it her way, it was as if she wanted as little to do with the wedding, and me, as possible. Considering the nature of our relationship up until then, I wasn't really surprised, but it still hurt terribly. Weddings are supposed to be happy times that draw families closer together. Although our wedding ended up being a great celebration, it was in spite of our families, not at all because of them.

Greg says: Except for God, we were pretty much on our own from the beginning. But we made it work. We got our bachelor's degrees, and I went to graduate school while we both worked starter jobs. We had to work really hard to stay afloat financially and emotionally. We were so poor that I had to use duct tape to cover the holes in the soles of my shoes, and several times a week (especially when we didn't have time to cook) we used to share a single-scoop ice cream cone for dinner. With only one car, we commuted together, so between our work and school schedules, we left the house at 5 a.m. and got back at 11 p.m. We were so exhausted we couldn't see straight. But as hard as it was, we prayed harder and held on to each other—and when that didn't work, we held on to our vows—for dear life. And we worked hard to learn what we didn't know, which, considering that we were so young with a ton of life being thrown at us faster than we knew what to do with it, was a lot.

In addition to the above, within the first five years of our marriage and between the two of us, we experienced a life-threatening illness, the loss of a baby, four job changes, two moves, two car accidents, a business start-up, and a partridge in a pear tree. (Okay, I'm kidding about the partridge. But everything else really happened.)

As we shared earlier, these might sound like difficult times. A lot of couples might even be put off by our story, thinking that if these are the kinds of things marriage can hold in store, who would want it? It's funny, but we don't really remember the early years of our marriage that way. In a lot of ways, these times were wonderful. We didn't have anything but each other and God, and that was enough. God blessed us with an incredible love, and when we were too tired, sick, or wrung out to do it on our own, God lent us some of his love, strength, and resolve to make up for what was missing. Almost twenty-five years later, we're still pretty much working hard, praying harder, and holding on to God and each other for dear life. Yes, along the way—and even in those first few years—there were many other terrifying moments that still make our heads spin to think about.

But there have also been wonderful, incredible blessings. As we clung to God and each other, our love grew stronger in so many ways. We fell more in love with each other because of how we took care of each other through the good times and the bad. We can honestly say that we don't know a single couple who is more in love with each other than we are. We have been blessed to experience a deep sense of rightness about our relationship, born of our mutual prayer life, that continues to sustain us through it all, combined with a commitment to nurture our love for each other especially when life gets hard or scary. And there are so many other wonderful things as well! We were blessed by: the children we eventually had both through birth and adoption and the incredibly intimate, inspiring, and fun family life we have created with them; the ministry God has given us and the many lives God has blessed both because of what we teach and the example he allows us to be to others; the many incredibly joyful and memorable celebrations of birthdays, anniversaries, and holidays that mark the many blessings God has given us. The home we eventually built, much of it on our own, gave us such a terrific sense of partnership and has become a symbol of the warm, loving life we have created together. The faithfulness we have shared though all the ups and downs of life has been a source of strength and confidence that we will always be there for each other no matter what. The love and joy we experienced and the things we have learned together about ourselves, each other, and life more than make up for any hardships. There isn't any question or hesitation about it. We would both do it all again—even the tough bits. We can honestly say that, thanks to God's grace, our marriage is truly an exceptional marriage that we have been both blessed by and that anyone would count themselves lucky to have.

The point is we really had everything going against us. When people justify their divorces by saying that they "were too young," "didn't have support," "didn't have a plan," "didn't have money," "faced too much pressure," or "got hit with the reality of life too hard and too soon," we are sympathetic. But we are also a living illustration of the piles of research that says none of these things matter when it comes to marital satisfaction and longevity.

Regardless of the path you took to your wedding day and the journey you're on now in the early years of your life together, we hope that the takeaway for you will be that if God could take two kids as young as we were, with as little support as we had and as little knowledge and plan as we had, and make something amazing out of our marriage (and our marriage is—thanks, literally, be to God—something truly remarkable), just imagine what God wants to do for you and can do for you. All of this came about just because we were faithful to him in our individual and collective prayer lives, unswervingly committed to our vows (even more so than to each other—though we are certainly committed to each other as well), absolutely committed to taking care of each other and being loving to each other even when we were tired or sick or stressed, and unhesitatingly willing to learn what we didn't know, instead of blaming our marriage or each other for being "broken" in some way.

When we share our story, some people, especially people who know us from the radio or our other books say, "But it's different for you. You're the Popcaks!" As if that means something. We're just two people who love God and each other. Just like you. There's nothing special about us. In fact, it's worth underscoring that we didn't come from ideal backgrounds. Greg's parents' marriage was fine, but it wasn't the marriage we wanted, and we've done a lot different than they did. Lisa's dad passed away from a brain tumor when she was five, and her workaholic mom never remarried, so there was no modeling in her home of what a great marriage or even a healthy family life looked like. Emotionally and psychologically speaking we started out with about the same "preparation" from our families of origin that anyone else has. The only thing that made us successful is that we fell into the four things that research shows distinguish couples who last from couples who don't. As we've shared throughout the chapter, couples who pray together and have shared meaningful spiritual commitments last longer and are happier than couples who don't. Couples who are committed to their vows more than their feelings for each other last longer and are happier than couples who don't. Couples who are committed to looking for little ways to make each other's lives easier and more pleasant even when they're scared, sick, stressed, or tired weather the storms of live better than couples who don't. Couples who aren't too proud to get skills when they hit tough times instead of blaming each other or their marriage are more likely to last a lifetime and experience more happiness in their marriage than couples who don't.

Your past—or, for that matter, your present—doesn't define your present or future. It is only the starting point of what will be, of what you will strive to become. Your current skill set (or lack thereof) doesn't define you. It only represents what you have yet to learn. And while it is good to have them, your best-laid plans most likely don't matter all that much, because life has a way of pulling the rug out from under those plans when you least expect it. When everything falls apart, it isn't the strength of your plan but your willingness to be flexible, creative, and committed to God and each other that will make all the difference in the world. As St. Francis de Sales put it in his *Introduction to the Devout Life*, "We trust the past to God's mercy, the present to our faithfulness, and the future to his providence." All that matters is putting into practice today the things that will help us love each other even better tomorrow, no matter what life throws at you in the meantime.

We started this chapter asking, "What does it take to create a great marriage?" Hopefully by now you can at least begin to understand that it isn't luck, that people aren't born to it, that there is no magic. Great marriages are not the result of good fortune or other accidents. Couples in great marriages simply practice certain skills and habits that lesser couples don't. More importantly, those skills and habits can be taught. You can learn them. By cultivating these habits and skills in the first five years, any couple—especially you—can establish the basis for long-term marital health and happiness.

God Has Great Plans for Your Marriage

St. Paul in Romans 8:31 says, "If God is for us, who can be against us?" The fact is that God wants you to have a great marriage. He wants your love to be the kind of great love story that people write books and songs and poems about and that young men and women pray to experience in their own lives. God wants this for you. People are often surprised by this. While everyone would like to have a great marriage, it has been our experience that many people have a tendency to think that working on a marriage is kind of selfish since they think it only benefits them. Because of that, a lot of people have a hard time imagining that God really cares all that much about them having a great marriage. But here's the thing. God really is rooting for you. He truly does want you to have a great marriage, because your marriage isn't just about you. It's about God and the Church, too. The shocking truth is God wants to change the world through your marriage!

> Marriage is actually a ministry, a way that we live out God's grace in the world so that he can bless the world and call everyone to him.

The notion that God wants to change the world through your marriage is revolutionary and it is a uniquely Catholic notion. The Church says that marriage is a "vocation." That means that marriage is actually a ministry, a way that we live out God's grace in the world so that he can bless the world and call everyone to him. But how can that be?

Diamonds Are Forever

A few years ago, there was a popular television commercial for a jewelry company. The ad showed an old couple walking in the park arm in arm. They were adorable. The little old man wore a beret, and though he was stooped with age he carried himself with a quiet strength. His wife held his arm tightly, and they both beamed at each other as the sun shone down on them. Then the camera cut to a young couple, also obviously in love, walking up behind the older couple. As the younger couple passed the older one, they exchanged knowing glances, and the younger couple looked at each other as if to say, "One day, we're going to be them. I want to love you that much when we're their age."

What does any of this have to do with God wanting to change the world through your marriage? Everything.

God created every single person with an ache in his or her heart for a love that doesn't fail. Every single person wants to believe that true love really is possible. Even so, sadly, in today's world, many, even most people, tend not to believe that it is really possible for them. According to a recent study, 67 percent of young couples are afraid of marriage either because they fear the pain of a potential divorce or because they are afraid they will be trapped in a miserable relationship.[6] In a world such as this, true love that lasts a lifetime seems like a fairy tale for many people.

But when others see couples who are making it, who are persevering despite struggles and personal imperfections, who are overcoming their challenges, who are working hard to learn the steps of loving each other, who are making it to "happily ever after," they can't deny that the love their hearts ache for is real; and they figure if it is possible for some, maybe it can be possible for them, too. Even more importantly, God uses that ache in our hearts for a satisfying earthly love as a way of pointing us toward his eternal love. After all, it can be pretty hard to believe that a perfect love from a God we can't see is possible if love between two flesh-and- blood people isn't. As Pope Benedict XVI put it, "True eros tends to rise in ecstasy toward the Divine, to lead us beyond ourselves." Of course, St. Paul said as much when he pointed out that marriage was a sign of the union that God longs to achieve with each of us (see Eph 5:31–32).

The point is, married life is an important ministry in the Church. Again, this idea surprises a lot of people. A lot of Catholics tend to think of "ministry" in terms of what they do at Church. They think they "minister" when they serve as a lector, sing in the choir, or serve as a sacristan or on various church committees. While these activities are all very important and beautiful ways we can serve God, the *most* important way Catholic married couples can minister is by working hard to have an incredible marriage. When you actively work on having the best marriage and family life possible, you give God an opportunity to show the world that a love that is freely given, total, always faithful, and fruitful is truly possible. Further, you give God a chance to evangelize the world though your marriage by bearing witness to the truth of the Catholic vision of marriage and family life. Too many people in the world believe that a love that doesn't fail is a fairy tale, that having children is a curse, and that marriage is an outdated, unhealthy institution. God wants to use your marriage to show the world, not only that it is wrong about all of those things, but also that he wants to give those things to everyone.

God wants to use the hard work you put into making your marriage the most joyful, loving, faithful, prayerful union on the block to show all people that he intends to satisfy the ache in their hearts for a love that doesn't fail. You can play an essential role in making that happen. We'll say it again: God wants to change the world through your marriage. Will you let him?

In the next several chapters, we will unpack the specific habits you will want to cultivate in order to have the kind of marriage that will make the angels smile and the neighbors want to know your secret. For now, it is enough to know that God has great plans for your marriage, and when you seek him together in prayer; commit to the marriage even more deeply than you have committed to each other; consistently work to do little things to make each other's lives easier and more pleasant even when you feel sick, stressed, tired, or fed up; and promise to learn whatever skills you need to keep growing stronger day by day; you can have the marriage of your dreams—a joyful, loving marriage that can last a lifetime and remind the world that true love really is possible when Christ is your strength.

CHAPTER TWO

Culture Shock

One of the first challenges a newly married couple faces in the first five years is the challenge of becoming a couple!

It doesn't matter how long or how well you think you knew each other before marriage. Saying, "I do," raises the stakes of your relationship in both wonderful and challenging ways. With this new level of "couplehood" often comes a dizzying number of concessions, compromises, and negotiations. When a man and woman get married, they bring all their traditions, expectations, habits, rituals, and routines they learned both on their own and from their respective families of origin with them. Couples are always surprised to learn how different they can be from each other even if they have the same faith, ethnic background, geographic origin, and education levels. Add even more basic differences to these common distinctions, and you have the potential of experiencing a whole cornucopia of conflict starters.

What Stage Are You In?

In addition to recognizing the many opportunities for conflict in the early years, it's important to realize that marriages tend to go through different stages. Each stage brings with it certain blessings and new challenges, and each stage requires the couple to learn new lessons in the school of love that is their home. Couples usually undergo the first three of the eight stages within the first five years. Below is a list of all eight stages and the challenges that come with each period of life.[7] We provided the entire list so that you can keep the whole picture in perspective as you look at these first five years. (*Note:* All time frames are approximate. Actual beginnings and endings of stages may vary greatly from couple to couple.)

1. Honeymoon Stage (0–6 months)

    Major goals: Establish strength and independence of your marriage.

    Individual goals: Foster intimacy and fidelity

2. Conflict and Negotation Stage (6 months–3 to 5 years)

    Major goals: Learn safe, effective problem-solving skills. Work out unique character of your relationship.

Individual goals: Maintain intimacy in spite of conflict.

3. New Pattern Stage (4–8 years)

   Major goals: Take time to let patterns negotiated in last stage take hold before starting too many other ventures.

4. Creative Stage (7–15+ years)

   Major goals: Maintain intimacy while pursuing goals that are important to personal fulfillment.

   Individual goals: Develop relationship with community at large. Increase potential for caring, nurturing, and creativity.

5. Homecoming Stage (14–25+ years)

   Major goals: Jettison unnecessary commitments for the sake of greater intimacy and time with family. Zero in on what's "really" important. Also, begin thinking about life after children leave home.

6. Launching Stage (20–30+ years)

   Major goals: Successfully launch children into the world. Answer question, "Now what?" about life and marriage. Midlife crises common.

   Individual goals: Maintain intimacy while figuring out what to do with second half of life.

7. Second Honeymoon Stage (30–45+ years)

   Major goals: Maintain intimacy, creativity, relevance in the world as late-midlife/later life is approaching. Find new ways to deepen intimacy and begin new projects that you didn't feel comfortable starting while children were still around.

8. "Happily Ever After" Stage (45+ years)

Major goals: Enjoy late years together. Confront loss and death. Maintain hope and meaning as end of life draws near.

Individual goals: Review life. Develop and pass on your wisdom.[8]

As we said earlier, we will primarily focus on the first three stages for the purposes of this book, but if you would like to learn more about the later stages of married life, please refer to our book *For Better . . . Forever!: A Catholic Guide to Lifelong Marriage.*

The Honeymoon Stage

This is usually a time of intense romantic feelings and excitement about the new life you are starting together. The Honeymoon Stage can last a few weeks to a few months, and it is a time when the initial excitement of deepening romance eases the experience of a multitude of emotionally loaded situations. The most important thing you can do in this stage is to begin establishing the habits of intentionally and regularly showing love, dating, praying, and working together.

It isn't enough to let these loving moments happen spontaneously. In order to get the full benefit of this stage (instead of merely enjoying it while it lasts), you also need to make them happen. That's because there will soon come a time when these things don't spontaneously occur anymore. It isn't that you no longer want to do these things; it's more that you won't have the time or energy to focus as much on your marriage as you do in the Honeymoon Stage. Pretty soon, other responsibilities and commitments are going to insist that you spend time on them, too. Learning to be intentional about carving out specific time to talk, pray, play, and work together—in addition to whatever time occurs spontaneously in this stage for these activities—is a major task of the Honeymoon Stage and will prepare you to deal more consciously and intentionally with the challenges of the next stage of marriage.

The Conflict and Negotiation Stage

Couples quickly move from the Honeymoon Stage to the less romantic-sounding Conflict and Negotiation Stage. In this stage, the couple faces the challenge of working out the ways they will handle all the big and small differences they have about the big and small activities of married life. What is the process we use to see that bills get paid? Who does the dishes, how, and when? What is the "right" way to set the table, celebrate a birthday, clean the house? What holiday traditions must you observe and which can you let go of? How do you deal with the in-laws? These are just a few examples of the kinds of challenges that hit couples full in the face in the first months and years. As you can see from the examples we offered, the conflicts couples need to negotiate at this stage generally break down into two categories: tasks of daily living and special celebrations. The recommendations we make at the end of this chapter will help you negotiate both types of conflict more effectively.

Managing the Emotional Bank Account

Before we give you some specific tips for dealing with
the two most common types of issues encountered in
the Conflict and Negotiation Stage, we want to talk
about how to take care of your overall relationship in the
middle of all this potential conflict. Many relationship
experts use the image of an "emotional bank account"
to illustrate why ongoing marriage maintenance is so
important, especially at times such as the Conflict and
Negotiation Stage. If you have a checking account, you
need to make deposits to cover the checks you write.
Likewise, in a relationship, the more loving things you
do for each other—giving compliments, offering small
acts of service, giving tokens of affection, sharing affection, being thoughtful, smiling at each other, and finding myriad small ways to make each other's lives a little
easier or more pleasant—the more you "deposit" relationship "currency" into the emotional bank account.
In the same way, the more difficult interactions you
have—arguing or facing problems, challenging each
other, asking each other to change something about
yourselves, asking one another to step outside what is
comfortable or familiar, or asking to do little things to
say "I love you"—the more you make "withdrawals"
from the emotional bank account.

The problem is the Conflict and Negotiation Stage
of marriage (which can begin as soon as the first few
weeks of marriage and can last for several years) is
chock-full of opportunities to make withdrawals and
less full of opportunities to make deposits, especially if
a couple tends to be more laissez-faire about maintaining their relationship. Research by the Gottman Institute

shows that couples who handle conflict best maintain a 20:1 ratio of positive to negative interactions when they are not in disagreement and a 5:1 ratio of positive and supportive interactions when they are disagreeing with each other.[8] For most couples, this takes real, conscious effort. The couple that tends to have a more easygoing, "we just enjoy hanging out together and don't like to make much of a fuss about anything" approach to their relationship will most likely be especially challenged in this stage because all of a sudden everything can feel like work. Like the Grasshopper in Aesop's classic fable "The Ant and the Grasshopper," this couple assumes that the good feelings that were spontaneously generated for them during the Honeymoon Stage will just keep going forever. They make no real conscious preparations for that time when things might not be so easy, and they end up surprised when the Honeymoon Stage starts packing its bags and Conflict and Negotiation knocks on the door intending to fill the vacancy.

At this stage, problem solving takes work. Maintaining the relationship so that it doesn't run a "negative balance" takes work. Replenishing the emotional bank account when it is "overdrawn" takes work. Being pleasant to each other when you're frustrated takes work. Carving out time and energy to go on a date can even take extra effort. This is often when couples are tempted to give in to the popular belief that "if we were in a good relationship, it wouldn't be so much hard work." This idea is a lie, of course, but it's a seductive lie. The truth is that learning to love someone more than yourself doesn't come naturally. We do need to work at it. And even when you do your best to try to show each other how special and important you are to one another, working out the different ways you approach daily activities (cleaning, paying bills, negotiating schedules and priorities, etc.) can still be a challenge.

ꝺU R S T O R Y

Greg says: We always did a pretty good job trying to be there for each other. Even when we were first married, we tried to make a point of carving out specific times to pray, date, and just talk. We wanted to make a point of being intentional about spending time together from the beginning. Even though we worked hard not to take each other for granted, figuring out the different ways we approached life was still a real challenge. When we were first married, we only had one car, so with our work schedules and my grad-school courses, we would often leave the house very early in the morning and get back really late at night. That didn't leave a lot of energy or time for chores, much less a relationship.

Lisa says: When Greg is stressed out, he cleans, or he at least likes to make neat piles of things. But when I get stressed, I tend to shut down and need rest. We even had different cleaning styles. He was fine just tidying up and surface cleaning, leaving the scrubbing and deep cleaning for "whenever we got to it." I liked to get it all done at once. I couldn't stand neatening up if I knew everything was filthy and gross underneath. All of this resulted in him running around straightening up the house at midnight when all I wanted to do was sit and cuddle and try to reconnect and recharge after a long, hard day.

Basically all the stress we were under in those early years led us to do what came naturally to us, and that sometimes made it difficult to sympathize with one another. I ended up feeling as if he was judging me for not doing enough, and he felt as if I was content to sit around and leave everything to him. We had a lot of arguments about that.

Eventually we developed a plan that worked for both of us. We carved out time each evening where we could just hang out and be close together. Knowing that we could make that time a priority really helped me be more open to him. It was great to feel as if Greg took my need for cuddle time seriously.

As far as the cleaning went, we made a deal that we would spend a few hours on Saturday mornings getting our house back in order. He'd sort of be the "advance team" and go through the room straightening and organizing since he was good at that (and I'd help as we got started), and I'd come up after him to do the polishing, scrubbing, and deep cleaning (and then he'd help me when he got finished straightening and organizing). We also made a deal that during the course of the week if he needed to tidy something for his sanity, he was free to do so. I was happy to help if he asked, but otherwise, I shouldn't assume he was mad at me for not keeping up with the house, and he shouldn't assume I was leaving it all up to him.

Over the years, he's gotten a lot better at the deep cleaning, and I'm a much better organizer. And we're both better at keeping up with things on the fly. Now we've learned from each other, and we can switch off pretty effectively. But in those early years, it really helped to define who was responsible for what and figure out a good starting point for learning how to get things done without stepping all over each other.

Dealing with Difference

In the previous section we described some of the challenges a couple might face in negotiating the day-to-day differences in the way they manage their lives, and we illustrated this with a story from our own marriage. Soon we'll offer some recommendations for negotiating these challenges more gracefully, but first we'd like to discuss the second type of difference couples encounter in the Conflict and Negotiation Stage: differences around holidays and celebrations.

Holidays and Traditions

In addition to the tasks of daily life, another area that leads to a lot of challenges in the Conflict and Negotiation Stage is how birthdays, anniversaries, and holidays are handled. Some people hate making a fuss about things while others love over-the-top celebrations. Some people prefer one or two small but meaningful gifts; others like a shower of presents. Some people are very specific that a birthday *must* be celebrated on the actual day; others are okay moving it to the weekend, and still others are fine with not celebrating at all.

Similarly, some newer-married couples have a hard time separating from the traditions they enjoyed with their families of origin and carving out their own traditions as a couple. Whether that involves where and with whom the couple has Sunday dinner, or where and how they spend Christmas or any other celebration in between, there is a huge potential for arguments. As you will see in our own story, it's important that couples take the time to learn about each other's backgrounds to really understand why various customs, traditions, and personal preferences are so important.

> **Lisa says:** I never really expected that two devoutly Catholic people as Greg and I were would have to negotiate culture shock around religious holidays, but we really did! Greg's whole family was Catholic and very into what I would consider over-the-top celebrations. His

mom didn't even like me that much but still bought a ton of presents for me at Christmas. Needless to say, celebrating holidays was really strange for me in the first couple of years of marriage.

One of the major reasons for this was that my family was not religious at all. My mom was raised Catholic, but in the worst way possible. My maternal grandfather, who was Protestant, promised to raise his children Catholic when he married my grandmother at the request of the Church. He was faithful to his promise in the sense that he made certain that my mom fulfilled her Sunday obligation, but that's all religion ever was: an obligation and an unpleasant one at that. She had to go to church because her father promised she would, but he remained largely anti-Catholic and there was certainly no discussion about how any of it related to God's love for her. As such, she rejected her faith as an adult. As I was growing up, I noticed that our Catholic faith was important to my dad, but he passed away by the time I was five, so we never went to church after that. I started attending church again because I had a crush on a boy who took me to his youth group, and I met a wonderful lady there who became a second mom to me. She helped me rediscover my faith. As a teenager, I would go to Christmas Mass alone and come home to a largely undecorated house. On Christmas day, we might exchange a present or two, but it was never a big deal. It was just another day off.

By the time Greg and I met in college, I was serious about my faith, but I didn't actually have any of the cultural traditions that usually go along with it. Instead, I was influenced by the Jewish culture that my mom sort of adopted as her own when as a child she lived in an apartment building full of Jewish families. Even though my mom never converted and never really got into the spirituality of it, we were regularly invited to Seders and Jewish holy days. By the time Greg and I got married, I was pretty well catechized about what Catholics believe and how we worship, but culturally speaking, I knew more about celebrating Passover as a family than celebrating Easter at home!

We worked hard to be generous to each other's traditions. For instance, Greg surprised me by asking to see my copy of the *Haggadah*, the book that described how to conduct the Passover supper. He read through it and offered to put together a Passover meal so I could stay connected to the celebrations that were important to me. For my part, I enjoyed learning about his family's holiday traditions and seeing how they came together around their celebrations. It was definitely an adjustment, but it was wonderful being able to learn from each other and create new ways of celebrating together. It was as if we were finding

ways to take the things that were old and familiar and make them fresh and our own.

The New Pattern Stage: Two Becoming One

Marriage is often thought of as two people becoming
one. As you move from the Conflict and Negotiation
Stage to the New Pattern Stage, you will come head-to-
head with the reality of daily life and how that com-
pares to lofty ideals. An easy way to think about it is to
consider when you as a child or adolescent experienced
growth spurts and with them, growing pains. Certainly
the pain was never fun and was oftentimes a challenge
on your little body, but in light of the fact that growing
pains are ultimately responsible for progress, the pains
seem less futile and more fruitful.

In the same way, the Conflict and Negotiation Stage
is the growing pains you will experience as two become
one, as "you" grow into "us." Rather than indicating
that something is wrong, the growing pains of the Conflict and Negotiation Stage represent that something is
very right. It can be painful, but it isn't a pain that tears
you apart. It is a pain that says your love is getting bigger and stronger. Here are some tips to keep in mind
that can help you address your inevitable differences
with generosity and grace.

I. There Isn't a "Right" Answer

There is a wonderful saying, attributed to St. Augustine:
"In necessary things unity, in doubtful things freedom,
in all things charity." In other words, we will agree to
agree on the critical matters of objective truth (such as

Church teaching), but in everything else, we respect our differences. The Conflict and Negotiation Stage is a good time to dust off that maxim.

The truth is there is no "one right way" to wash the dishes, do the laundry, or celebrate Christmas. It can feel as if there is, or should be, but there isn't. There may be suggested "best practices" or good ideas about how to do these tasks well, but they aren't gospel. You can't turn to page X of the Bible where God says, "Behold, let it be decreed to the Israelites from henceforth the toilet paper must dispense over the roll, so sayeth the Lord your God." And you can't turn to page Y of the catechism to learn that "lest he clean the family room before he cleans the kitchen—let him be anathema (i.e., excommunicated)!" Because these issues aren't related to matters of fact or even revelation, most of the items you will be negotiating at this stage in your marriage are not "necessary" but rather "doubtful" (i.e., matters of preference); therefore, you should try your very best to exercise some generosity in the way you approach these tasks. The "right" way to do all of these things is not the way you were raised to do them or even the way you might personally prefer to do them, but rather the way that will work for the two of you in the context of the life you are living now. In the early years of marriage, the harder you cling to ways you used to do things or the ways you personally prefer to do things, the harder a time you are going to have. Being generous about these matters means first asking, "How can we approach this task (whether a daily task or a holiday celebration) in a manner that respects the lifestyle,

the time, and the energy we actually have?" Then act
accordingly.

2. You Are Not Losing Yourself

In the early years of marriage, many husbands and
wives feel that they are "losing themselves" because of
all the changes they have to make. They can feel that
all the things they are familiar with, all the things they
know and love, are changing or being taken away. That
can be very sad and very painful, and it is more than
okay to grieve these changes in appropriate ways (i.e.,
any way that doesn't alienate your spouse or turn you
into an angry, self-centered partner).

At the same time, it will be important not to confuse
your identity (who you are) with what you are familiar with. Changing your morning routine, for instance,
might feel uncomfortable and unfamiliar, but that is different than saying that changing your morning routine
is causing you to lose your very identity. Toddlers, not
adults, build their identities around their preferences.
The average three-year-old is not a child who prefers to
eat peanut-butter sandwiches with the crusts cut off; he
is the child who can only eat peanut-butter sandwiches
with the crusts cut off, and how dare you suggest otherwise! The toddler's emerging identity is so new that
it needs to latch on to external preferences to stabilize
itself. All of us need to work to get past this tendency to
falsely confuse what we like with who we are.

The truth is, while it is difficult to let familiar things
go, we actually find our true selves by doing so. What
does that mean? Well, if we are not the man or woman
who must do the laundry this way or else, then who

are we? According to the Church, we are the people who discover ourselves by living out all the virtues that enable us to live life as a gift and by being generous to each other through mutual love and service (see *Gaudium et Spes* and *Evangelium Vitae*). When we respond graciously to our mate's preferences, and even better, work together to discover new ways of doing things that respect our current state in life (rather than clinging to the old one), we are practicing the virtues that help us discover who we truly are, the virtuous people God created us to be.

The Church tells us that we actually find ourselves by making a gift of ourselves.[9] When you generously surrender the past and comfortable ways you used to do things so that you can learn new ways that actually respect the life you are creating instead of the life you left behind, you are actually discovering who you really are—a person created by God to be virtuous, good, generous, and loving, a person who is capable of choosing to love someone more than you love your own comfort zone. Admittedly, this is not an easy thing to do, but it is always an admirable thing to do, and it is exactly what having a great and truly joyful marriage (especially a great, joyful, *Catholic* marriage) requires you to do. Moreover, the quicker you can make it to the New Pattern Stage, overcoming the petty tendency to cling to preferences, the happier you will be you did it!

3. Listen to Each Other

When faced with your partner's preference to do something differently than you would prefer, the most common reaction is to behave as if they are insane. "What's wrong with you? Why would you want to do that? (Or, "Why would you want to do it that way?")

Obviously, that approach leaves most people cold. Here's a tip. When your mate wants to do something that you don't, or wants to do something in a way that differs from your preference, don't react to what they want. Instead, seek understanding. Respectfully ask why they want to do that (or why they want to do it that way). Don't ask why in an accusatory sort of way. Rather, try to understand the reasoning behind the desired goal or approach. For instance, you might say, "It never occurred to me to do X that way; why does that work best for you?" Or you might say, "I've never done that before. Can you help me understand what that means to you?"

> When your mate wants to do something that you don't, or wants to do something in a way that differs from your preference, don't react to what they want.

By taking this approach you can learn about the benefits your partner imagines might result by doing that thing or doing it that way. If you do this, one of two things will happen. Either you will come to see the value in their opinion and agree with them, or (more commonly) you can brainstorm alternative ways (i.e., ways that are more comfortable to you) to get the same benefit.

For instance, imagine that your husband wants to pay the bills on a weeknight. You're tired after work, and you'd rather wait until the weekend. Most couples would then just argue back and forth about whose idea was better, and they would either be forced to give up (because there's no way to win an opinion-based argument), or the person who was the most stubborn would win (ultimately resulting in the other partner harboring a pile of secret resentments).

But let's say this couple read *Just Married* and decided to use our suggestions to try and understand each spouse's thinking. Instead of setting up a polarizing argument in the face of her husband's desire to pay the bills on a weeknight by criticizing, when she is too tired to deal with it, the wife (let's call her Sophie) says, "Can you tell me more about why you feel it's important to do this tonight?"

The husband (we'll call him Aaron) says, "Because if we don't get them done by next Monday we're going to get hit with late fees. Plus, I don't want to have to do any more work over the weekend. I'd rather just be able to relax."

So now Sophie is presented with a choice. She can either see the wisdom in her husband's point of view and agree to pay the bills together that night even though she's tired, or she can suggest an alternative that would address Aaron's concerns (i.e., avoiding late fees and enjoying the weekend). Let's say she's still not ready to give up her night in the tub, and she'd like to propose another option. "I definitely understand wanting to avoid the late fees and not wanting to have to do more work on the weekend, but I'm still pretty tired tonight. How about this: what would you say if we saved the bills for Saturday morning when we're fresh, but I can pick up those pastries you like at the bakery and make a nice breakfast? We can put on some music and just hang out while we pay the bills together. We don't have to be anywhere until two o'clock anyway, so that might be a nice way to get things done and get some time together. If we did the bills tonight, I'd probably just be grumpy anyway. This way, I get the night off tonight, we still get to avoid the late charges, and we get a nice, relaxing breakfast out of the deal. What do you say?"

At this point, Aaron can agree to Sophie's proposal, in which case they might have just established a new pattern, "paying bills over Saturday breakfast." Or Aaron can propose an alternative that takes Sophie's ideas and concerns into consideration. For instance, he could suggest that she take the night off, let him just take care of the bills this month, but they could still get together for breakfast on Saturday.

Whatever the couple ultimately decides is beside the point. For our purposes the process this couple uses to arrive at their new pattern is the most important issue. Instead of just arguing back and forth, "Pay the bills now!" "No, pay them this weekend!" "No, pay them now!" and so on, Sophie and Aaron are brainstorming new ideas to meet each other's concerns so that they eventually arrive at the perfect solution, a solution that satisfies them both and probably will become the new pattern this couple follows—consciously or unconsciously—to pay bills in the future.

This process can work to help you solve just about any opinion-based argument. Remember these steps:

1. Instead of reacting, ask questions to understand the benefits your mate thinks his or her approach will achieve.

2. Now that you know the benefits, you can either choose to agree with his or her plan or . . .

3. Propose any number of alternative approaches that give your spouse the same benefits but in a manner that is more respectful of your needs or concerns.

Practicing these steps can help you grow in the generosity that lies at the heart of a great Catholic marriage, and it can help you get through the Conflict and Negotiation Stage that much more quickly.

4. Don't Agree Just to Get Along

This tip might seem counterintuitive. After all, if the goal is getting through the Conflict and Negotiation Stage as quickly as possible, and you don't really care all that much about what color the bathroom should be or whether you go to your family's house for dinner this weekend, why not just agree?

Often, this can be perfectly fine, as long as the outcome really doesn't matter that much to you. But beware of the tendency to agree just because you don't want to create drama, which is followed at some point down the road by a resentment that bubbles up from inside and poisons the love in your marriage.

Too many people buy into the idea that "you shouldn't sweat the small stuff and everything is small stuff." Again, there's no need to create a fuss if something really doesn't matter to you, but there are two things to consider. First, your spouse probably still wants your intelligent input on those decisions, whether you care about them or not. Your world might not turn on whether the bathroom is painted Ostrich Egg White or Country Snow White, but being part of the process communicates that you care about the things that are important to your spouse. That always feels good, and it's a great way to show both your love for your partner and your investment in the marriage.

Second, too many people tell themselves that everything is small stuff . . . until it isn't. They harbor the resentments we described above, but they never say anything about them because "it's just stupid stuff. It shouldn't matter." It doesn't matter whether it should matter to you or not. If you're disturbed by it, it does matter (whether it should or not), and you need to find a way to respectfully say your piece. Most of this "Oh, why bother?" attitude is really borne out of a fear of conflict that tends to lead to much bigger conflicts later on. Even if you don't really care about the outcome of a particular situation, walk through the process we described in point 3 above. Ask questions that draw out the reasoning and benefits behind the different options your spouse is presenting. At worst, your husband or wife will think you're a fantastic listener who always knows just the right questions to ask. At best, you might just find out that you care more than you thought, and now you have a way to make sure your needs are represented respectfully.

Pray Together

Finally, in a Catholic marriage, couples are called to "be subordinate to one another out of reverence for Christ"

(Eph 5:21). In other words, Christ is the head of your home. Anytime you are trying to decide the best way to approach a task or celebration, you have to ask him, together, what to do.

If you haven't ever prayed together, don't worry. The next chapter is dedicated to developing that skill. Right now, we just want to drive the point home that if something is worth arguing about, it's worth praying about even more.

There is nothing that is too small to ask God's help. As you discovered in chapter 1, God wants you to have a great marriage so that he can show the world how to love. Learning to love each other in the big things and the little things allows you to perfect the dance of intimacy. Let God show you the steps of the dance he created.

> If something is worth arguing about, it's worth praying about even more.

Moving On

If a couple makes good use of the ideas we've outlined in this chapter, they will most likely move through the Conflict and Negotiation Stage within the first three to five years of marriage—give or take. The New Pattern Stage, which blends into the tail end of the Conflict and Negotiation Stage and continues until the new challenges of the next stage, the Creative Stage (raising children, new career challenges and opportunities, purchasing or building a family home), makes the couple dust off the skills they learned in the Conflict and Negotiation Stage and apply them to issues of greater complexity. Ideally, the New Pattern Stage represents a brief pause in which the new patterns established for handling daily tasks as well as special celebrations can "set up" like the concrete poured for the foundation of a house.

That said, life tends to be a bit messier than these stages can suggest, and often bits of the Conflict and Negotiation, New Pattern, and Creative Stages exist at the same time. The way you run your daily life might be in the New Pattern Stage while the way you handle birthdays could still be in Conflict and Negotiation. Or maybe you are starting to negotiate the Creative Stage as you have your first child, but you're still struggling— through a fair amount of Conflict and Negotiation—to find the balance between your marriage and your families of origin. Don't worry. The point of this chapter is not that everything has to be tied up in a neat package. What we really want you to take away is that conflict in the early years—even a fair amount (and certainly more than you want)—is perfectly normal; that this is this time to learn to deal with your differences respectfully; and that if you pursue mutual understanding, respect, and solution-focused discussions over rigid self-preservation, anger, and emotional accusations, you'll be just fine no matter what the world tries to throw at you.

Just to be sure, the next few chapters will give you additional critical tools to help make your marriage as strong, loving, joyful, and passionate as it can be so that your relationship will not just stand the test of time, but it will ace it.

CHAPTER THREE

The Couple Who Prays Together

"The family that prays together,
stays together."

Fr. Patrick Peyton, C.S.C.

We've mentioned the idea of couple prayer several times throughout the book. The idea of praying together as a couple can strike many Catholics as awkward if not downright offensive. Many Catholics have been raised to mistakenly believe that prayer is a private affair that is simply too personal and too intimate to be shared with one's spouse, but nothing could be further from the truth. As Catholics, we believe that while prayer is

certainly an intimate affair, and deeply personal, it is
never private.

Prayer is always a communal activity. Catholicism
gives us a myriad of examples for communal prayer:
Mass, the sacraments, benediction, Stations of the Cross,
and so on. Even when we confess our sins, which ought
to be the most intimate and private sort of prayer, we
confess them to another person who, in prayer, helps
us bring them to God and conveys God's forgiveness
to us. By definition, prayer is an activity that draws us
into deeper intimacy with God and others. While there
is certainly a place and a time for praying on your own,
there is really no such thing as a prayer that you keep
to yourself. As the catechism tells us, "Prayer is Christian insofar as it is communion with Christ and extends
throughout the Church, which is his Body."[10]

If a couple truly wishes to live a full and joyful Catholic marriage, praying together is anything but optional.
The good news is couple prayer isn't just good for you
as a Catholic; it's good for you as a spouse, too!

Science Says—Benefits of Couple Prayer

Although as Catholics we recognize the benefits of
prayer as a matter of faith, there is a surprising amount
of research on the relationship between couple prayer
and both marital stability and marital happiness.

For instance, a joint study by the University of Virginia and the University of Texas at San Antonio found
that up to 83 percent of couples who pray together are
happy with each other and their marriage compared to
only 69 percent of couples who do not pray together.
In fact, ruling out demographic factors such as race

and income levels, couples who pray together tend to be about 15 to 20 percent happier than couples who don't. Likewise, research by the Florida State University Family Institute shows that couples who pray together display higher levels of marital commitment and are significantly less likely to fall prey to infidelity.[11] These are just two examples of literally hundreds of studies that consistently show that when couples worship together, pray at home together, and actively encourage each other in the practice of their faith, they are dramatically more secure and happy with each other than couples who don't. In fact, according to sociologist Andrew Greeley, of all the factors known to contribute to marital happiness and stability, couple prayer has been found to be "the most powerful correlate of marital happiness that we have yet discovered."[12]

The More the Merrier

Building on this body of research, the Baylor University Institute for Studies of Religion wanted to know if how much couples prayed together made a difference. What they found was close to miraculous. Couples that prayed together more frequently were up to 30 percent more likely to endorse positive statements about their spouse and their marriage than couples who prayed together less frequently. Take a look at this breakdown of the research found in the book, *Couples Who Pray*, which shows the difference of agreement with positive statements between couples who pray together "sometimes" (A) versus couples who pray together "a lot" (B).[13]

Do you agree with the following statements?	(A) "We sometimes pray together." (%)	(B) "We pray together a lot." (%)	Increase (%)
"Our marriage is happy."	60	78	18
"My spouse is my best friend."	74	91	17
"We both try to make our marriage better."	65	86	21
"My spouse makes me feel important."	59	77	18
"My spouse delights in me."	39	69	30
"We have very good agreement on finances."	58	69	11
"Our agreement on basic values is very good."	72	83	11
"We are greatly satisfied with our family life."	38	54	16
"We agree on how children should be raised."	64	75	11
"My spouse is romantic."	41	63	22
"My spouse is a skillful lover."	48	65	17
"We feel spiritual after lovemaking."	49	68	19
"We can both peacefully disagree."	66	75	9
"We are very confident in our marriage."	76	92	16

As you can see, in every case, couples who prayed together frequently thought better of each other and experienced their marriages to be more stable, joyful, and passionate. God really does want you to have a great marriage—so much so that when you pray together he personally teaches you how to do it!

 Prayer Habits Quiz

Try taking the following quiz with your spouse to find out how your prayer habits are affecting your relationship.

How often do you pray together?

Sometimes ❑   A lot ❑

Do you agree with the following statements?	Yes	No
"Our marriage is happy."	❑	❑
"My spouse is my best friend."	❑	❑
"We both try to make our marriage better."	❑	❑
"My spouse makes me feel important."	❑	❑
"My spouse delights in me."	❑	❑
"We have very good agreement on finances."	❑	❑
"Our agreement on basic values is very good."	❑	❑
"We are greatly satisfied with our family life."	❑	❑
"We agree on how children should be raised."	❑	❑
"My spouse is romantic."	❑	❑
"My spouse is a skillful lover."	❑	❑
"We feel spiritual after lovemaking."	❑	❑
"We can both peacefully disagree."	❑	❑
"We are very confident in our marriage."	❑	❑

Couple Prayer: Where to Start?

It doesn't matter whether you are a beginner to prayer (both as individuals and as a couple) or if you are individual prayer masters. Every couple can learn to create a meaningful, enjoyable, and intimate prayer life together. As you get started, we'd like to suggest a few things that might help newcomers to prayer in general and couple prayer in particular overcome nervousness or squeamishness.

1. Relax

Many people who are newer to personal or couple prayer are a little intimidated because they feel that it has to be a *big deal*. They're afraid that they have to kneel ramrod straight and use a lot of "thee's" and "thou's" and keep everything very formal and proper.

Nothing could be further from the truth. Jesus says, "I no longer call you slaves, because a slave does not know what his master is doing. I have called you friends, because I have told you everything I have heard from my Father" (Jn 15:15). God calls you his "friend." If you want to know how to talk to God, think a little bit about how you talk to your friends, and do that. For some people, this feels a little odd. After all, isn't God the King of the Universe? Absolutely, he is. But if the King of the Universe asks you to be his friend, wouldn't it make sense to take him at his word? God loves you. He wants you to tell him about your life, your joys, your struggles, your concerns. He wants you to invite him into the everyday events that define your life and marriage. Jesus says, "Behold, I stand at the door and knock" (Rv 3:20). Won't you open the door and let him into the heart of your marriage?

To begin praying, especially praying as a couple, go where you feel comfortable. If you would like to kneel, that's great, but sitting together on your couch or lying in bed is okay, too. (Just try not to fall asleep!) If a friend was coming to visit you, you would probably try to make your home as comfortable as possible. In the same way, the place you pray, the posture you choose, and the way to think about talking to God should all be focused on helping you relax and be comfortable in the presence of the God who moved heaven and earth to be a friend to you.

2. What Do You Say?

Just like when you're with a really good friend, don't get nervous about saying "the right things" and having to pray "the right way." There is no more a right way to pray than there is a right way to talk to a friend. When you are with a friend, sometimes you complain about things and sometimes you talk about all the great stuff that is happening in your life. Sometimes you ask for help, and sometimes you tell your friend how much you appreciate that they are in your life. Sometimes you talk about your marriage, sometimes you talk about your life, and sometimes you don't talk about much of anything at all—and those can even be the best times. Sometimes you laugh, sometimes you cry, and sometimes you even get angry. Believe it or not, it's okay to tell God when you are angry at him. Trust us. He's a big God. He can take it. Better yet, he will help you sort it out and make it better. At any rate, he would rather you tell him when you're angry than keep it to yourself and let it become a barrier. Remember, he calls you "friend." Don't let anything come between your friend-ship with God any more than you would let anything come between you and your best friend.

3. Keep It Up

Prayer, especially couple prayer, gets easier the more you do it. The trick is to keep it up. Don't get discour-aged if you find that, especially at first, you struggle to be consistent about your prayer time. That's called being human. It can be helpful to pick a specific time (say, 9 p.m.) or at least a particular time period (after dinner, right before bed, etc.) so that you can establish a couple-prayer ritual. The more you stick to your time, the quicker you can learn to be comfortable with prayer and experience the power of a praying couple.

4. Encourage Each Other

Even though trying to stick to a regular time is ideal, don't get discouraged if you forget for a day or two, or even a week or two. For example, it would be easy for a couple to give in to the temptation to become angry or resentful if the husband or wife felt as if the other was "dropping the ball" when it came to initiating prayer.

Try to remember that while it's the job of both of you to make prayer happen, the most important thing is that it happens. Once you develop a regular habit for couple prayer, you can always improve on things by doing a better job of switching off who takes the lead or discussing the different ways you might like to pray together—but those improvements can only happen if you've already established the habit. Make sure you are patient with yourselves and each other, especially when you begin. It's tough to learn a new habit. God understands. Don't argue over whose "job" it is to make prayer time happen, and don't keep score of how many times you initiated prayer versus how many times your spouse brought it up. Just make it happen. (In fact, this is a good general rule for a healthy marriage.)

5. Be Supportive

Everyone prays differently. God is happy to receive our prayers however they are said. Be careful not to criticize each other or laugh about the way your mate prays. Hopefully, you wouldn't think of shaming or making fun of your spouse—ever—especially in front of a good friend. Adopt the same supportive, encouraging, positive attitude as you're learning to talk to God, who wants to be your best friend.

Now that we've looked at some of the attitudes you and your spouse should try to cultivate to make couple prayer a positive experience, let's take a look at how you might actually begin to pray together.

Couple Prayer: What Do You Say?

So, you've managed to get together at a good time and in a good place, and you're ready to start praying together. Now what? The short answer is: whatever you want.

Because there isn't a right way to pray, you have a lot of freedom about what your prayer time might look like. That said, here are some things you might like to keep in mind so that you and your beloved can get the most out of couple prayer.

1. Remember the Point

No matter what you do, always remember that the point
of couple prayer is not about checking off certain boxes
or jumping through certain spiritual hoops. At its best,
couple prayer is a shared, intimate conversation with
God that brings you closer to him and to each other.
Keep thinking about what kinds of prayer might have
the greatest chance of helping you accomplish those
ends. If you're not sure, we'll give you some resources
that can help you figure things out, but for now, don't
be afraid to engage your creativity. Do you have a favorite prayer from childhood? A particular devotion, such
as the Rosary or Divine Mercy Chaplet, that you'd like
to try? Is there a scripture study guide or prayer book
you're familiar with or that someone has recommended
to you? Maybe you're just more comfortable talking to
God in your own words out loud. Feel free to experi-
ment. It's normal to feel awkward the first few times
you try to pray together as a couple, but if you find that
you feel as if you're always doing the same old thing
(and that's not doing anything for you), or if you keep
feeling empty or bored, try a different approach. The
beautiful thing about our faith is that there are so many
ways Catholics can pray; you'll never run out of options.

2. Formal or Informal Prayer?

There are two basic forms of simple prayer: formal and
informal. Formal prayer involves prayers that have been
written by the Church; the Hail Mary, the Our Father,
the Rosary, a scripture study, and other devotions are
some examples. Formal prayer isn't formal in the sense
that it's fancy and requires you to wear a tuxedo or ball

gown, but in the sense that it follows a particular form. We like to think of formal prayer as a love poem or a love song. Even though someone else wrote it, singing "your song" to each other or quoting lines from a meaningful passage of a favorite poem can be a beautiful way to share your heart with someone you love. In the same way, using different types of formal prayers can be both a great way to get started with couple prayer (because it eliminates the guesswork) and a great way to go deeper (because you are praying with the mind of the Church). Some of the greatest couple prayers began with something as simple as a nightly commitment to say one Hail Mary or Our Father together for "the intention of our marriage."

That said, it would be a little odd if, when you wanted to tell each other how much you loved each other or say something important, you only sang love songs or quoted poetry. You need to talk to each other in your own words, too. In fact, it's all the personal conversations you've shared and all the meaningful moments you've created together that give those songs and poetry their power. That's why informal prayer (that is, prayer in your own words without a predetermined form) can be an important part of couple prayer, too. Formal prayers can become most meaningful when they help you recall all the times you've shared your heart with God in your own words. If you're not used to praying in your own words, you might begin with some simple statements such as, "God, thank you for X" or, "God, please help me (us) with Y" or, "Please bless my friend so-and-so." You don't have to be flowery or even wordy. Just put your heart into it as you would in any really good conversation with a really close, mutual friend, and let things develop from there.

3. Take Turns

For some people, the most intimidating thing about couple prayer is figuring out who says what and when. Be casual about this. You can even work it out while you pray by looking at each other and asking, "Do you have anything you want to say or add?" The normal way couples approach figuring out who says what and when is by simply taking turns. For instance, one of you might say the first half of the Hail Mary (up to ". . . the fruit of thy womb, Jesus"), and the other might say the second half (Holy Mary . . . hour of our death, Amen."). Or, you might spend a minute or two thanking God for the blessings of today in your own words, and then, before you move on to whatever the next part of your prayer might be, you might stop and give your spouse an opportunity to thank God for something in his or her own words. Once both of you have said your piece, you can move on to the next part of your prayer time. Like learning a new dance, with practice, you'll be able to be more flexible about who says what and when, but for starters, taking turns responding to each part of your prayer can be a great way to kick things off.

4. Think about Your Goal

Each time you pray, it can be helpful to think a little bit about the different reasons people pray and what you hope to take away from your prayer time. For instance, sometimes we pray to thank God either for a particular blessing or just for being God and loving us. Sometimes, we ask God for help for us or a friend who is suffering. Other times, we need to ask God for his forgiveness and his help not to let us commit the same sin again. It can be good to think a little bit about what is the most important thing to communicate to God today. If you're stuck, that's okay, too. Just tell God that you're not sure what to say, and ask him to put the words he'd like you to say into your heart. Sometimes the best prayer times come when words fail us and we just let the Holy Spirit do all the work in us. Regardless, when a couple prays together, it can be good to start your prayer time with a brief discussion about what you'd like to take from the experience. You don't have to have a spiritual plan ready for filing in triplicate with the home office. Just chat enough to have some idea of what the point of your prayer time is—for example, thanking and praising God, asking for help or guidance, asking God to bless someone whom you know is in need, asking forgiveness for some struggle, or some combination of all of the above. Knowing what you both hope to take from your prayer time can help couple prayer be a more positive experience.

5. Be Flexible

Some nights you'll have more energy and time than others. It's okay to vary your prayer time from day to day. Perhaps one day you can only manage to say a Glory Be. The next time might be the same. The following day you might pray in your own words together. The time after that, maybe you'll want to pray a Rosary, and the next day you might be back to the Glory Be. Making the commitment to regular couple prayer is more important in the long term than how you pray on any given day. Just try to build on what you usually do as time progresses. Learning the process of prayer—especially couple prayer—is more of a journey than a destination. Make sure that over time you are moving deeper into the journey with the way you pray. No matter how simply you start out, you will find that in time, with a regular commitment, God will take you deeper in his own time and as you are ready. Trust him. In fact, that's one of the most important parts of the process.

The PRAISE Format

When we pray together, we follow all of the suggestions we've made above, but something else that has been very helpful for us is having a semistructured prayer time. Depending on how much time or energy we have on a given day, going through all the steps of the format can take five minutes or it can take an hour. There are no rules.

That said, many couples who pray together find that they get the most out of it if they spend a little time with each of the different reasons people pray (praise, penance, petition, discernment, intercession). Because of that, we like to use the acronym PRAISE to serve as a guide to our couple-prayer time.

P   Praise and thank God for his blessings.

R   Repent of the small ways you've let God or each other down.

A   Ask for God's help with special concerns that are on your heart.

I   Intercede for others.

S   Seek his will about bigger decisions or questions you are facing.

E   Express your desire to serve him until you meet again in prayer.

As we indicated above, this format could take five minutes or an hour, and it can include elements of both formal and informal prayer as you see fit. Over the next few pages, we'll take a look at each step and give you a brief example of what it might look like in practice.

P - Praise God

Take a moment to thank God for the times you've felt his presence in your day or for the little blessings you've experienced. Don't feel as if you have to say anything fancy. Just take turns between you and your spouse thanking God for the ways he has shown that he is taking care of you. For instance,

> **Greg says:** "Thank you, Lord, for letting me get my project done in time for the meeting today and helping it go so well."

> **Lisa says:** "Yes, Lord. And thank you for helping me find that great sale at the grocery store. Thanks for helping us keep to our budget."

> **Greg says:** "And, God, I just want to thank you for letting my wife and I get some time for a date this weekend. Thanks for giving us the time we need to take care of each other."

As we said, this doesn't have to be fancy. You can thank God for everything from the great parking spot

> God doesn't need our praise, but when we praise him, it reminds us of all the little ways he is present in our lives and it enables us to trust him more.

you got close to the mall entrance to the miraculous recovery your mom made from that illness. Big or small, it doesn't matter.

Some people feel silly thanking God for "stuff that just happened" or "stuff I did," as if those things had nothing to do with God. God is the source of all good gifts. If you had a moment where you felt grateful today, bring it before God and thank him for it—together. Being thankful is a simple way of giving God the praise he deserves. God doesn't need our praise, but when we praise him, it reminds us of all the little ways he is present in our lives and it enables us to trust him more. Plus, couples spend so much time complaining to each other about things, it can be important to take a few moments to celebrate your successes—even the little ones. Finally, taking a moment to recall the things one is grateful for is good for your mental health. One study showed that the simple exercise of listing the things one is grateful for increases one's level of happiness by 25 percent.[14] Happier spouses make for happier marriages!

R - Repentance

We're not talking about confessing your sins here. You can save that for confession. But this would be a good time to reflect together on the little ways you might not have done as good a job taking care of each other and to ask God to help you do better the next time similar circumstances arise.

> **Greg says:** "Lord, I'm sorry for being short with Lisa when I got home from work today. She really didn't deserve it. Thank you for not letting it turn into a 'thing.' Help me to do a better job taking care of her when I feel frustrated about my work."

> **Lisa says:** "And, Lord, I'm sorry for not trying to be more understanding. I know that he wasn't really upset with me, but it's hard not to react. I'm grateful too that you gave us the grace to not turn it into an argument, but help me to be more understanding and sensitive next time."

Keep in mind that this PRAISE format is just a guideline. You don't have to use all the steps all the time (or at all). Some days you might not feel as if you have anything to repent of, but most days, there will probably be something you'd like to do better or get God's help with. Admitting your simple flaws in front of your spouse and God requires humility—but so does having a great marriage. Letting God, and your spouse, know of your commitment to do better next time is a great way to keep those resentments from building up. Plus, God will give you the grace to overcome those weaknesses so that, in time, they won't be weaknesses anymore.

A - Ask

This step comes fairly easy to most people. We're good at asking God for things. Take a moment to ask God for help with any practical concerns you might have. They don't have to be particularly noble or spiritual concerns. Just invite God into your everyday life, and let him know that you know you can't do anything—even the smallest things—without him.

> **Greg says:** "Lord, please help me to get everything done. I feel really overwhelmed by all the things going on right now, and I really need your help clearing my head so I can get on top of it all."

> **Lisa says:** "Yes, Lord. Please help Greg have a peace about all he has to do, and help me be a good support to him. Also, Lord, please help me get over this cold quickly. I'm really feeling run down, and it's really hard to be the person I want to be when I feel like this."

> **Greg says:** "And help me to be sensitive to the fact that she's feeling poorly and find ways to take care of her and let her know how much I love her."

As we showed in the example above, when you can, don't just ask God for help with the specific concerns; ask him to give you the wisdom and grace to be there for each other and support each other as you address those concerns. God wants you to be each other's helpmates. Let him teach you how to do it, and ask him for the grace you need to follow through.

I - Intercede for Others

Don't forget to pray for the people in your life who have special needs or concerns. Take a moment to not only ask him for his grace and blessing on them, but also to ask him to give you the grace and wisdom you need to find ways to be a blessing to those people whenever possible.

> **Greg says:** "Please bless Chuck. Help the doctors find out why he keeps having those migraines and make him well. Help me not to be resentful when he has to take time off and I have to cover for him. Help me to support him through this."

> **Lisa says:** "And, Lord, please bless Ann at church. She is having such a hard time with her son. Help her know how best to deal with him, and help me be a good friend to her through this tough time."

Interceding for others in this way not only calls God's grace down on those loved ones who need it; it also reminds us of our dependence on God and helps us remember that he wants us to be his blessing to those in need.

S - Seek

This is similar to asking for God's help, but it has to do with bigger concerns that might take a little longer to figure out what God wants you to do about them. Learning the steps of hearing God's voice (i.e., "discernment") is beyond the scope of this book (for more information on this, check out our book, *The Life God Wants You to Have*[15]), but suffice it to say that when you consistently ask God for his advice and counsel, he will find ways to get through to you. When you're Christian, everything doesn't have to be up to you anymore. God wants to help. And when you seek God's will together, God will speak to both of you so that you can check each other's math, so to speak.

> **Greg says:** "Lord, Lisa and I aren't really sure if we should start looking for a new house. We're starting to outgrow this one, but everything is so expensive. Help us to know your will, whether that is to stay here or to go somewhere else. Find us the home you would want us to raise your children in, and even though I'm nervous about looking at homes, please give me the wisdom to know what's really best for us and the courage to do your will, whatever it is."

> **Lisa says:** "Yes, Lord, help us to really know what you want. And even though I really want to move, help me to be sensitive and considerate to Greg's concerns. Help me to be open to all the ways you want to provide for us. And let us work well together as we try to understand what you want us to do."

In addition to asking God to let you know his will, make sure to bring your desires to him in a way that says, "This is what I would like, but your will, not mine." The good news is that even when God's will is different from yours, it will still make you happy. He made you, after all. He knows better than anything else what it is going to take to make you authentically happy. Don't be afraid to pray for his will.

While you're at it, as we showed in the example, when you and your spouse are of different minds about a bigger decision, ask for God's grace to be sensitive to each other's concerns and to find ways to be a support to each other as you find your way forward. This will go a long way to preventing those arguments where you each stake out an opposite position and then just verbally hammer away at each other until one of you—resentfully and angrily—surrenders.

Couple prayer is especially important when you're seeking God's will about any decision that affects your marriage and family life (which is pretty much everything, when you think about it). We regularly talk to couples who pray individually about such big decisions, but come to different conclusions in their prayer time. For instance, a wife says that, in prayer, God is telling her it's time to have a child (or another one) while the husband says that God is telling

> When you and your spouse are of different minds about a bigger decision, ask for God's grace to be sensitive to each other's concerns and to find ways to be a support to each other as you find your way forward.

him to wait. What's going on here? Is someone lying? Is God sending mixed messages?

Assuming that both the husband and wife are sincerely seeking God's will, even if they are coming to different conclusions in their prayer, it may not be that one is mistaken, and it is certainly not that God is sending mixed messages. What we usually find is that God is showing the husband and wife different pieces of the same puzzle, but the husband and wife are mistaking their piece for the whole picture. For instance, in the example above, it may be that God is showing the wife that it is time to have another child, but he is showing the husband that it will be important to overcome a challenge in the marriage, such as with a child they already have, as a way of clearing the road for that next child. It isn't that God is saying yes to two different and mutually exclusive ends. Rather, God is giving the husband and wife different pieces of the same puzzle and then asking them to exercise their communication and couple-prayer muscles so that they can learn to be better helpmates to each other as he teaches them how these two different pieces of the puzzle fit together.

E - Express Your Desire to Serve Him until You Meet Again in Prayer

This is basically where you wrap up. Couple prayer shouldn't just be limited to the specific time that you are sitting together praying. Because your marriage is a sacrament, your whole marriage is a prayer. God wants to use everything that happens in your marriage as a way of opening your hearts to him and to each other. Because of that, it's a good idea not to just end your prayer and put it away as if it was a piece of exercise equipment. Instead, end your prayer with the understanding that God wants to keep reaching out to you both throughout your day. Ask him to help you be attentive to what he is trying to tell you so that the next time you meet in prayer, you have more to share, more to be thankful for, and more questions to put before him. This way, your whole married life can be the prayer that it is because your whole married life can be an ongoing conversation with God.

> **Greg says:** "Lord, thank you for this time together. Help us to know what you're saying to us through the things that happen in our lives and all the movements of our hearts. Help us to always put your will first."

> **Lisa says:** "Yes, Lord. We love you. Let everything we do reflect that love for you and each other, and keep us safe until we can meet you again together in prayer. Amen."

Concluding your prayer in this manner helps prepare your hearts to receive whatever God might wish to share with you, and it makes you mindful that God wants to spend every moment of everyday with you—not just prayer time. When you wrap up your couple-prayer time with a request to stay open to the movement of the Holy Spirit, you begin to make a personal connection to the idea that married life is, itself, a prayer. It helps you see the truth in what Archbishop

Fulton Sheen once said, that "every moment is pregnant with divine purpose."

Although the PRAISE template is largely a guide to informal prayer, some couples get a great deal out of adding formal prayers to it. For instance, you might open your PRAISE time with an Our Father to get things started and close with a Hail Mary or Glory Be. Some like to follow their time in PRAISE with a Rosary, Chaplet of Divine Mercy, brief scripture reflection, or other meaningful devotion. The point is this is your prayer time. You should feel free to do whatever makes this time more meaningful to you and your spouse. Just remember to be generous to each other. If something is meaningful to your spouse but maybe not so much to you, open your heart to the possibility that God might want to reach out to you in some new ways. Rather than turning up your nose at a prayer or type of prayer that is meaningful to your spouse, be generous and learn from each other. You'll be glad you did as you give God even more avenues to bring his grace into your own heart and your life together.

Some Closing Thoughts

Throughout this chapter, we've showed you some of the basic steps of praying together as a couple, and we've shared some of the benefits we have encountered in our own lives together and in the lives of other couples we've helped learn how to pray together.

If you thoughtfully consider the suggestions we've made in this chapter, you might begin to see why couples who pray together really are happier in their marriages than couples who don't. If you pray together daily, especially using the PRAISE format we outlined, you can see that your prayer doesn't just draw you closer to God; it also puts you in a different mindset about your marriage. It makes you more generous. It makes you more considerate. It helps you be more aware of each other's concerns. It helps you reflect more deeply and meaningfully on how you might be able to support each other through those cares and concerns. It gives you a simple way to deal with and heal from those little ways you might have disappointed each other. It can help soften your heart so that when you disagree, you can still leave a little part of yourself open to the possibility that you might be wrong, or that God wants to show you an even better option. And, of course, it can help remind you both of the little ways God is taking care of you every day and enable you to truly stop and celebrate—even if only for a moment—these little blessings of each day that make life, and married life in particular, worth living.

You'll receive that (and more) in as little as about ten minutes a day!

There is one more benefit we have found to praying together this way. As you enter into the Creative Stage of marriage (the stage after the New Pattern Stage when life starts to get filled with career and responsibilities of family life), conversations between a husband

Establishing couple prayer as a ritual in the early years of marriage will help you maintain that critical connection through the Creative Stage years.

and wife can be reduced to brief exchanges about shopping lists and whose turn it is to bus which kid to what event. Taking ten minutes or so every day to have a meaningful prayer time can give you a shortcut way to learn what is in each other's hearts and to discover ways to hold on to each other when life is pulling you in three million different directions—and it's only Tuesday.

Establishing couple prayer as a ritual in the early years of marriage will help you maintain that critical connection through the Creative Stage years. So many couples don't realize they need a ritual such as couple prayer until they are already flying apart at the seams from overcommitment, and then they try to retrofit prayer time into their marriage, only to discover that adding one more thing just isn't humanly possible.

Marriages tend to build on precedent. The habits you establish now will most likely set the tone for many years to come. Building your marriage on a foundation of prayer is like being the man in scripture who builds his house on a foundation of stone (Mt 7:24–27). Nothing can shake such a house. It will provide shelter, comfort, safety, and warmth for years to come.

John 12:36 says, "While you have the light, believe in the light, so that you may become children of the light." Remember, God wants to change the world through your marriage. Making a commitment to couple prayer will enable you to let the light of Christ shine brightly in your hearts and in your home. Your love for each other will be warmed in its glow, and you will be a light to the world that is aching for the love God is showing you—day by day—how to live.

CHAPTER FOUR

The Four Stages of Conflict

Nobody likes conflict, but as you've seen so far, the early years of marriage offer plenty of opportunities to experience it. Even so, this doesn't have to be an intimidating or even unpleasant reality. There is actually a way to disagree with each other, deal with those disagreements, create solutions together, and come out on the other side feeling more in love with each other because of the conflict rather than in spite of it. Does this sound like a fairy tale? If so, read on, because in the next few pages, we're going to share some phenomenally powerful and practical ideas that can help you make this "fairy tale" come true in your marriage. By the end of this chapter, you'll have the skills you and your spouse need to slay the conflict dragons that threaten your marital peace in the early days and begin working toward your own personal, "happily ever after."

Conflict: What It Is and What It Isn't

There isn't one way to argue effectively, but there are some things that couples need to keep in mind that can help them resolve their differences more efficiently. Likewise, there are some bad habits that must absolutely be avoided in order to have the kinds of marital disagreements that help you love each other more because of those disagreements instead of in spite of them.

Research by the Gottman Institute identifies four bad marital communication habits that the researchers actually refer to as "the four horsemen" (after the four horsemen of the apocalypse in the Book of Revelation) because of their power to undermine marital peace, love, safety, and trust. These habits tend to be progressive in the sense that one habit taking hold leads to the next habit emerging, and so on. Together, they represent the four stages of marital-communication collapse: Criticism, Defensiveness, Contempt, Stonewalling.

Criticism

Every couple complains about things in their marriage. Believe it or not, complaining about things in your marriage can actually be a positive and healthy activity. But when complaints become criticisms, that's when the first stage of marital-communication collapse begins to threaten your ability to solve problems together and feel good about each other in conflict. What's the difference?

A complaint is just an observation that either a need is not being met or things are not the way you would like them to be. Complaints simply and respectfully call attention to problems you would like to solve.

IDENTIFYING COMPLAINTS EXERCISE

The following are examples of complaints. Put a check mark beside the types of complaints that you hear in your home a lot.

❑ "I'm so tired of getting to church late on Sunday!"

❑ "We really need to find a better way to keep up with the housework. This is killing me."

❑ "We're spending so much time with your family. I like them, but I could really use some time for 'just us.'"

❑ "I know you have a lot of work to do this weekend, but I miss you. I'd really like it if we could find some time for each other. The last couple of weeks have been really tough!"

In each of the above examples, the complaint represented the way one spouse called the other's attention to a problem that needed to be addressed. The complaint was nonpersonal, nonattacking, and thing focused (i.e., it addressed an event or situation that needed to change).

Criticisms, on the other hand, are very personal, usually attacking, and spouse focused.

IDENTIFYING CRITICISMS EXERCISE

Let's look at the same four situations we presented above, but this time, we'll state them as criticisms. Put a check mark beside the kind of criticisms that are common in your relationship.

❑ "You take *soooo* long getting ready! I'm so sick of waiting around for you every Sunday. You know how much I hate being late for church!"

❑ "Why do you always leave all the housework to me. You're so selfish! Did it ever occur to you that maybe I'd like to have some down time once in a while?"

❑ "God! What is with you and your obsession with seeing your family all the time? It's as if we can't get away from those people! Don't you think it might be time to cut the cord?"

❑ "You're such a workaholic! You never have any time for us. You probably wish you never got married. You sure act like it."

As you can see, in each case, criticism takes the focus off the problem and makes your spouse the problem. Sometimes (as in the example of time with family of origin) criticism obscures the real problem (the lack of couple time) altogether.

In order to solve a problem in a marriage, you need your partner to "buy in." That is, you need your spouse to agree that there is a problem and get them to invest in solving it with you. Because criticisms are basically personal attacks, they don't tend to generate agreeable offers of help from your mate. What they do generate are angry, defensive responses that focus on shifting blame, deflecting attacks, and never actually getting around to figuring out what the real problem is, much less solving it.

> In each case, criticism takes the focus off the problem and makes your spouse the problem.

REACTIONS EXERCISE

Review the following reflections, which are commonly thrown around in the face of criticism:

- "*I* make us late? If you're in such a hurry, why don't you actually help for a change instead of surfing on the computer all morning?"

- "You act as if I don't do anything around here! I can never make you happy!"

- "What did my family ever do to you! Why do you have to be so mean? They actually like being with us. How terrible! Geez, most spouses would kill for in-laws like that!"

- "Do you have any idea of how stressed I am right now at work? Everything's coming down on me, and all you can do is complain about your needs not getting met. How about thinking about someone other than yourself for once?"

Each of the above responses, as unpleasant as they are, are completely natural and utterly predictable reactions to the criticisms we listed above. That's not to say that if your spouse criticizes you, your defensive responses are justifiable or excusable. We can never justify our bad behavior by appealing to our spouse's missteps. But even so, using criticisms instead of complaints to voice your concerns almost always ends in disaster.

What to Do

If you keep getting caught in the criticism trap, practice the following suggestions.

First, when you feel a criticism coming up (you can usually hear the irritable comment forming in your head before it comes out of your mouth), literally say to yourself, "Stop. This kind of thinking doesn't help me get my needs met."

Second, pray for a gentle spirit (1 Pt 3:4), ". . . the hidden character of the heart, expressed in the imperishable beauty

> ...the hidden character of the heart, expressed in the imperishable beauty of a gentle and calm disposition, which is precious in the sight of God. 1 Peter 3:4

of a gentle and calm disposition, which is precious in the sight of God." In that moment, offer up a quick prayer to ask God to help you choose your words carefully and to bring up the problem in a way that enlists your spouse's support instead of antagonizing your partner. It doesn't have to be fancy, but instead can be simple. "Lord, I want to kill him. Help me be thoughtful and sensitive in the words I use to bring this up."

Third, ask yourself what the problem actually is. For instance, is the problem getting to church late, or is the problem really figuring out how to work better together so you can get there on time? Is the problem really seeing your in-laws, or is it actually more about working together to find time for your marriage? If so, lead with that.

This is usually about the time when people inevitably ask us, "Well, what if it's both?" In other words, what if it is both how much time you spend with the in-laws and how little time you get with each other. In those cases, it's still always better to lead with the most important of the two needs. After all, if you're figuring out how to spend more time with each other, you've automatically got less time to spend with the in-laws.

These suggestions are obvious if you take a minute to think about what you're really upset about. The problem is most of us don't stop and think before we open our mouths. When you're upset about something, taking a minute to calm down, gather your thoughts, and choose your words isn't just about being nice to your spouse. It spells the difference between setting up a conversation that will help you get your needs met and setting up a conversation that will make you feel resentful.

One last thought: everyone criticizes their spouse once in a while. It's never great, but it's normal, and most relationships can tolerate the occasional slip into criticism. But if criticism marks the normal, habitual, and automatic way you talk to each other, then you have officially entered the Criticism Stage of marital-communication collapse. You need to make changes. Now. It will only get harder from here if you don't. Start with the suggestions contained in this book and in the classic *Why Marriages Succeed or Fail* by John Gottman. It might also be time to attend a marriage-encounter weekend so that you can learn some new and more respectful ways of communicating. Likewise, a few sessions of couple's therapy at this stage can make all the difference in the world. You might think it's silly to start looking for a marriage counselor when divorce is the furthest thing from your mind, but don't wait until you hate each other to learn new skills. If you can identify small problems while they're still small problems and get the skills you need to overcome those issues, then you can become marriage masters despite the bad habits you might have picked up along the way. And you can cultivate those skills before you're in a make-it-or-break-it situation. When it comes to marriage maintenance, a stitch in time really does prevent the whole marriage from coming apart at the seams. Check out our resource chapter for more information on help for conquering criticism.

Defensiveness

The second stage of marital-communication collapse is Defensiveness. That's when spouses get to the place where almost any time something even remotely negative comes up—even in the most innocent way possible—it provokes either a "Don't blame me!" or "What about you?" response from you or your spouse. For instance, imagine that you are frustrated that your car payment wasn't made on time. You mention it, you think, in a fairly respectful way to your spouse, but the response you get surprises you, "What? Is your dialing finger broken? Am I the only one around here who can pay a bill?"

Let's take another example. Let's say you can't find your keys. You're searching through drawers, and you mutter under your breath to yourself, "Where the heck did my keys go?" Suddenly, your spouse pipes up out of the blue, "Don't blame me! I didn't take them!"

In the above examples, even though you didn't necessarily blame your spouse for not paying the bill, or stealing your keys, your spouse felt attacked. That could either be because your marriage has spent so much time in the Criticism Stage that now even benign comments provoke a defensive response, or it could mean that your spouse was raised in a home that was generally antagonistic and is now primed to react to everything defensively. Either way, it's a bad habit, and it must be broken.

Defensiveness is problematic because it takes the focus off the problem to be solved and makes the conversation all about protecting "my dignity." Now, all of a sudden, you're not looking for your keys, but you're having an argument about whether you really respect your partner or not.

When you feel those defensive urges bubbling up inside, first say to yourself, "Stop. My spouse is just stressed about something. Don't react."

Second, pray, in that moment, for a spirit of understanding and helpfulness. Understanding and helpfulness are the antidotes to defensiveness.

Third, say something understanding or helpful. For instance, "Would you like some help in sorting out the bills?" or, "Is there something I can do to help you find your keys?" Say it as sincerely as you can manage, even if you don't feel it inside. Feelings follow actions. If you can commit to acting in an understanding and compassionate way, you will begin to feel the defensiveness give way to feelings of understanding and compassion.

Saying something that is understanding or helpful short-circuits the Defensiveness Stage, lowers the emotional temperature of the discussion, and makes it possible to solve the problem at hand. But does that mean that you should let your spouse get away with speaking to you in an antagonistic way? Of course not. That wouldn't be loving. After all, if loving someone means working for their good, you owe it to your spouse to give him or her a chance to handle their frustration more charitably in the future. Later, once the problem is solved, you might go back and process the discussion so that you can handle things better next time. For instance, you might say, "Hey, Hon, remember when you thought I threw away your paperwork? Would you mind just asking me for help next time instead of accusing me? It would mean a lot." Saying this when your spouse is still frustrated about the paperwork is useless, but going back to it after you have helped find the paperwork and discussing how to handle similar situations in the future can help you leave behind defensiveness for good.

Again, as with the Criticism Stage, every couple is defensive with each other from time to time. That's normal. But when defensiveness is easily provoked and becomes the habitual, expected reaction to even mildly negative exchanges, your marriage has entered the second stage of communication collapse. The resources in the previous section about criticism are even more important at this stage. The good news is that with a little attention, any couple can leave defensiveness behind and cultivate a more helpful and understanding relationship.

Contempt

The third stage of marital-communication collapse is Contempt. Contempt includes any comments that make another person feel small. Contempt can involve abusive behavior like name-calling and humiliation, but more often it involves subtler ways of saying, "I'm better than you." Any time you make a comment using a tone that puts an unspoken "you idiot" at the end of the sentence (for instance, "We've talked about this a million times (you idiot)!"), you are being contemptuous. Correcting your spouse about "what really happened" or correcting your spouse's grammar in the middle of an argument—as one woman we know was in the habit of doing to her husband—are other examples of behavior that could be contemptuous depending on the tone and context.

When a couple gets to the point where they have come to expect a defensive response to whatever is said, a lot of hurt has built up inside the couple. Because of that, every time an issue is raised, even in a charitable way, it can tap that reserve of anger and pain that's always just below the surface. When that pain comes out, it is expressed as contempt. The spouse who gives in to the temptation to be contemptuous isn't really trying to hurt his or her mate. What he or she is really trying to say is, "I'm hurting, and I don't know what to do about it." That said, it can be difficult to remember this when you're in the line of fire.

> The spouse who gives in to the temptation to be contemptuous isn't really trying to hurt his or her mate. What he or she is really trying to say is, "I'm hurting and I don't know what to do about it."

When couples reach the Contempt Stage of marital-communication collapse, there are a few things they need to do. First, pray in the moment for a spirit of compassion. Compassion—the realization that your spouse is hurting, not hostile—is the antidote for contempt. Ask yourself, "What pain could possibly be motivating these words and actions?" (Note: this does not apply to behavior that is physically threatening or violent. If you feel threatened by your spouse at any level, don't excuse this behavior. Seek professional help immediately.)

Second, don't address the contemptuous things your spouse said. Don't defend yourself. Don't react in anger. Don't dignify the comment. Instead, validate the emotion behind the words, and redirect toward solutions. For instance, if your spouse calls you a "jerk," don't argue about whether you are or aren't a jerk, and resist the urge to return the insult with one of your own. Instead, say, "Look. I see how angry (hurt, upset, anxious, sad, etc.) you are. But yelling at me (calling me names, etc.) isn't going to fix anything. What do we need to do right now to help you feel as if I'm on your side so we can fix the problem together?" This is not going to come naturally to you. Feel free to use your own words, but regardless you're going to need to rehearse this so that you're ready to go the next time the contempt comes. Write it down and review it every day.

All that said, couples at the Contempt Stage are often beyond self-help. With appropriate support, almost every couple can recover and rediscover their love and compassion, but it almost always requires professional assistance. There are two avenues we'd recommend. First, Retrouvaille (reh-TROO-vie, "Rediscovery") is a wonderful marriage-support program led by other couples who have faced the brink and made it back. The Retrouvaille program is held on weekends with six follow-up meetings that can give tremendous assistance to couples who need to learn how to make communication safe and productive again. Visit www.helpourmarriage.com or contact your local diocesan family life office for more information.

Second, couples at this stage should also take advantage of professional marital counseling. On average, couples struggle on their own for four to six years before seeking help, and they can do a lot of damage to each other and the relationship in that time period. The terrific news is that marriage therapy has come a long way in the last few years. Success rates for marriage counseling are in excess of 90 percent for even the worst-off couples if they are working with a trained, marriage-friendly therapist. (Note: many counselors will say that they "do" marriage counseling but are often not trained. Make sure that your therapist has training and supervised experience in marital counseling and is pro-marriage). Two resources for marriage-friendly counselors are www.marriagefriendlytherapists.com (for local referrals to trained, competent, pro-marriage therapists) and www.exceptionalmarriages.com (the website for our telephone counseling service where you can work with a trained, Catholic marital counselor with regular sessions over the phone). Additional resources are included in the back of this book.

Stonewalling

The last stage of marital-communication collapse is Stonewalling. Once contempt takes hold of a marriage, some husbands or wives—and sometimes both spouses—just stop participating in discussions altogether. Asking almost any question, especially questions that could hold the potential for disagreement, can result in stony silence from your partner. Sometimes a spouse might pretend not to hear. Sometimes the spouse will just get up and walk out. Other times a spouse might just stare blankly or change the subject. Regardless, the upshot is that the person who initiated the conversation feels rejected, frustrated, and abandoned.

Truth be told, the stonewaller isn't trying to be mean. He or she genuinely believes he or she is doing the best thing. After all, if most conversations end badly, then one can get to the point where it is easy to believe that the best way to "save" the marriage is just by not having conversations. Of course, this is a serious mistake.

Research shows that marriages in the Stonewalling Stage are at a critical juncture. More than 90 percent (according to some research) of couples who reach this stage and seek marriage-friendly, professional help can recover and go on to have a terrific marriage. That said, a very high percentage of couples at this stage who do not seek help will divorce within five years.

The takeaway for readers is that while it may be true that couples in the Stonewalling Stage may not have the skills they need to make it on their own, they can learn to love each other and celebrate married life once again. It can be hard to admit that a couple needs help, but as Proverbs (11:2) says, "With pride, disgrace comes; but with the humble is wisdom." Couples at this stage can begin to get the help they need by reaching out to the organizations we mentioned in our discussion on contempt.

CHAPTER FIVE

Managing
Conflict
Gracefully

We spent the last chapter talking about the bad habits you need to avoid and reviewing the habits you need to cultivate instead. For instance, complaints (nonpersonal, nonaccusatory statements about needs or concerns) are fine; criticisms (personal, antagonistic blaming statements) are not. Understanding and helpful statements can defeat defensiveness, and compassionate statements can overcome contempt. Knowing when you need help and having the humility to seek that help can make all the difference between becoming a marriage master or being a marriage disaster. And prayer, before and after conflict and especially during—both as an individual and as a couple—is critical to successful, godly, marriage-building communication. Having reviewed some of the specific traps couples fall in, we'd like to offer seven additional tips to help you successfully resolve conflict.

1. Take Care of Each Other

Ironically, the most important thing about problem solving has nothing to do with actually solving the problem. The most important thing about resolving problems is a willingness and commitment to do whatever it takes to make your partner feel taken care of while you work together to solve the problem.

Think about it. What happens if you feel neglected, attacked, demeaned, or disregarded by your spouse? You get defensive. You stop listening. You return slight for slight. As mentioined before, research by the Gottman Institute shows that couples who handle conflict well maintain a 20:1 ratio of positive to negative interactions outside of conflict (e.g., doing thoughtful things for each other, smiling at each other, sharing affection, saying, "I love you," etc., versus ignoring, taking each other for granted, picking on each other, "forgetting" or neglecting to do thoughtful things, etc.) and a 5:1 ratio of positive to negative interactions while they are in conflict!

The last part of that statement sounds crazy to many couples. How do you manage to be positive and supportive during conflict? Can you never disagree? Obviously not. It's just that couples who are good at problem solving know that the best way to get through a difficulty is to work with their partner to solve the problem instead of treating their partner as if he or she is the problem. Especially when a couple is discussing difficult topics, little things can go a long way.

RATIO EXERCISE

Circle the phrases that feel the most natural to you, and remember them for the next conflict between you and your spouse.

"Thanks for hanging in there with me."

"I really love you, you know."

"I'm okay with taking a break if you need to think about it a little."

"Can we just take a minute to pray about this?"

"My throat's a little dry. I'm going to the kitchen to get a drink. Can I get you something?"

"I know this is hard. I really appreciate your making the time to talk through this with me."

"I'm really serious about finding some solution that will make us both happy."

"I know there aren't any easy answers to this one. What can I do to help you feel as if I'm on your side while we work all this out?"

"Why don't we take a walk (or do some other activity) while we talk about this?" (Having an activity to focus on while discussing difficult topics can diffuse some of the tension and stop you from noticing and reacting to every eye roll or grimace your spouse makes.)

These are just a few examples. You should feel free to use this list as a springboard for your own creativity.

The point is that when we disagree with our spouse, it can be easy to get so caught up in what we want and how we feel that we behave as if only our agenda matters, and not our spouse. But when we are made to feel as if we don't matter, we have a tendency to put up roadblocks to effective problem solving. The harder you work to make each other feel taken care of, even when you disagree, the quicker you will resolve your disagreements.

2. Identify, Pray, Solve

The best way to approach a conflict with your spouse (or anyone for that matter) is always with an open mind, open soul, and open heart. When you do this, you prepare yourself to work together with your partner in life to come to an agreement that works for your marriage. The best way to ensure that this happens is to go in with a game plan, and we recommend adopting the model of identifying the problem, praying about the problem, and solving the problem.

a. *Identify the real problem.* Too often, the thing we're upset about isn't the problem we really need to solve. Maybe you're mad that your husband left his socks on the floor, so you yell at him about that, but the real problem is that you need more help around the house in general. If you just yell about the socks, the larger problem is going to be missed. Maybe you're mad about your wife buying that expensive pair of shoes, but if you just yell at her about that, you're missing an opportunity to solve the real problem—the need to get a budget you can both agree on. Before you open your mouth to complain about the latest offense or the most recent irritation, take a minute to ask what the real problem is.

b. *Pray about the best way forward.* Once you've decided what the real issue is, take a moment to ask God to help you figure out the best way to address the problem. Sometimes, you might be surprised to find that the best thing to do is just let it go. After all, some problems do solve themselves with a little patience, understanding, and time. Of course, if you find yourself still being irritated about something after you've tried to let it go, it's definitely better to bring it up. That said, praying about the problem before you speak about it will remind you that God has a stake in how this problem is addressed and will connect you with the grace you need to discuss your problems with charity and respect.

c. *Identify a possible solution and lead with that.* Once you've identified the actual problem and taken it to God, try to think of how you might like to solve the problem. If you can lead with a possible solution instead of leading with your emotions, you'll have a better chance of success. For instance, which of the following statements do you think will have a better chance of setting up a good discussion about a problem?

"You're so thoughtless!"

vs.

"I'm really tired and I could use some more
help to get the house in order. Could you get
your schedule so we could figure out a time to
get the bedroom cleaned up?"

"I can't believe you would talk to me that
way—and in front of our friends!"

vs.

"I really need us to figure out a better way
to handle those times when we get on each
other's nerves in public. What would it take to
save those conversations until we get home?"

"Your mother is a total witch!"

vs.

"I need your help figuring out a way to handle
your mom when she tells me that I've gained
some weight. Ignoring her doesn't work. What
can I do or say that won't upset you, but still
lets her know that I'm not open to discussing
certain things with her?"

Obviously, in each case the second statements have
the greater potential to be successful than the first.
Equally obviously, the second statements are not the
sort of thing one just says in the heat of the moment.
Many people believe that in order to be "true to themselves" they are obliged to say what they are feeling
in the middle of feeling it, but the truth is, feelings
are God's gift to you, not anyone else. Your feelings
are God's way of calling your attention to a potential

problem. Having received the emotional message, you need to go to God to figure out whether the emotional message was a glitch (because you were tired, or under-fed, or overwrought, or otherwise not functioning prop-erly) or whether it was intended to point out some real issue that needed to be addressed. Having sought God's counsel and calmed down a bit, now it's time to raise the issue. Instead of leading with your emotions, lead-ing with possible solutions gives you a way to discuss possible ways to prevent the situation from occurring in the future without letting the conversation devolve into "I feel so awful about who did what to whom."

3. You Don't Have to Agree on What "Really" Happened

The couples we talk to on our radio program and in our counseling practice often get hung up on the question, "How can we solve our problems if we can't even agree on what happened?" These couples get stuck arguing so much about the details of who did what to whom and when and how that they never get around to solving the problem. Let us let you in on a little secret. It is a very rare instance, indeed, when any married couple—espe-cially the best ones—actually agree on what "really" happened. Agreement about who was wrong and who was right and who started it and how happens once in a while, but it's certainly not the norm. Take it as a gift if it happens, but don't count on it.

The good news is that to solve a problem, you don't actually have to agree on what happened, because it will probably never happen again exactly the same way. All you have to agree on is that neither one of you was pleased with how things went down and that you both would like to see things play out differently the next time. Then you can begin the conversation by simply saying, "The next time X happens why don't we handle it this way instead of what we did last time?" The conversation can continue from this point, not with rehashing old wounds, but with kicking new possible solutions back and forth until you can agree on something that will work for both of you.

4. Watch Your Temperature

Almost everyone knows that it's not a good idea to let your emotions run away with you. The problem is most of us are lousy at noticing our emotions are running away with us until we've already run that marathon and are collapsing, exhausted, in the middle of our wreckage. Smart couples know how to gauge their emotional temperatures and take action to get control of themselves before things get too hot.

Imagine an "Emotional Temperature Scale" that runs from one to ten. The breakdown would look like this[16]:

10. Raging (physical abuse often ensues)
9. Fuming (yelling, name-calling, verbal abuse)
8. Furious (Accusatory Statements and Defensiveness)
7. Angry (time to take a break)
6. Stressed Out
5. Mildly Stressed
4. Calm and Focused
3. Relaxed Engagement
1-2. Total Relaxation

1–2. Total relaxation: You're on a beach (metaphorically speaking) without a care in the world.

3. Flow: A state of relaxed engagement where you are caught up in the moment and hyperfocused on what you're doing but still completely relaxed.

4. A really good, normal day: Even though there are some challenges, you are calm, focused, and relaxed. At a 4 you have the experience of remembering what you like about being you and doing the things you do.

5. An average day: There are ups and downs, and you sometimes have to work a little harder than you might like to keep up with your stress, but overall, things are fine.

6. A stressful day or moment: You can be outwardly civil and solution focused, but inwardly, you're struggling to pull it off. There is tension in the air between you and others, even if it is unexpressed (verbally). You're still on top of things, but it's now taking real effort to stay there. Stress chemicals (such as cortisol and adrenaline) are starting to flood your bloodstream and ramping up the very beginnings of your fight, flight, freeze-up response.

7. The outer limit of effective problem solving: At this stage, most people would deny to themselves and others that they were angry. This is the "I'm fine! What?" stage. At this level you can still problem solve, but if the person you are talking to does one more stupid thing (in your estimation), all bets are off. At this level, the cortisol and adrenaline have built up enough that the nonverbal filters in your

brain (the filters that stop you from looking visibly annoyed at people) are starting to collapse. Eye rolling, heavy sighing, tsk-tsking, fidgeting, and nervous energy that needs to be expressed through cleaning, pacing, and other mildly obsessive acts start coming out at this stage. You do not ever want to exceed this stage in any conversation. This is when you need to take a break. Any later is going to be too late.

8. The first time most of us are willing to admit (to ourselves or others) that we're upset: At this point, the build-up of stress chemicals in your body has caused the nonverbal filters in your brain to completely collapse, and now the verbal filters are under assault. Your logical brain is literally beginning to shut down, and your emotional brain is beginning to take over. You might appear calm on the outside, but your heart rate is upward of 120 beats per minute (it's around 80 at rest), and your body is experiencing many changes that will prevent you from being effective. You aren't at the name-calling and yelling stage . . . yet. But you are at the stage where you have now stopped trying to solve the problem and started exclusively trying to figure out how to blame the other person for the problem (or get them to shut up and go away). This is the first outward sign your fight, flight, freeze-up response has been engaged. Most couples don't even start a problem-solving conversation until they get to this level, and then they must discuss the issue—right now. A much better course of action would be to

follow the "identify, pray, solve" process we outlined earlier.

9. The verbal filters in your brain have completely gone offline: You are yelling and screaming (or you have shut down and can't think or talk). Name-calling and intentionally hurtful comments may be forthcoming. Abandon ship! Initiate emergency "must stop now" procedures!

10. Physical filters are falling: Doors are being slammed and objects thrown—Alternatively, if you tend more to flight than fight, you may be shutting down completely and, possibly, not wanting to speak for days until you can calm down again. At worst, arguments are becoming physical in some way. This is a catastrophic level that couples should never allow themselves to reach. Much damage can be done to a relationship that is not easy to heal without professional help.

The point of this scale is to help you see what behaviors are associated at each stage so that you can know when it is appropriate to initiate a conversation and when it is necessary to disengage no matter how much you feel as if you want to keep going. A good rule of thumb is never engage in a difficult conversation until you have gotten yourself down to at least a 6 or lower, because the conversation is probably going to raise your emotional temperature by at least two points. If you start at a 7 or higher, you have no place to go but crazy.

5. Take Breaks, Early and Often

As we mentioned above, everyone knows the importance of taking breaks, but almost everyone takes them
too late, resulting in scenes where, at about an 8, one
spouse proclaims, "I'm not talking about this anymore.
I'm done!" and the other responds, "Like hell you are!"
and then they follow each other around from room to
room trying to, loudly, not have the conversation.

In order to work, a break must be taken much earlier, say at around a 7. At this stage, breaks are brief
moments when one spouse or another steps away from
the discussion to collect themselves so that they can
shortly return to and continue with the conversation.

For instance, let's say that you're feeling as if you
or your spouse is at the 7 on the emotional temperature
scale. To take a break you might say, "I'm sorry, my
throat is really dry. Do you mind if I grab a drink? Can
I get you something while I'm in the kitchen?" Or even,
"I'm sorry, I need to use the bathroom. I promise I'll be
right back."

While you're out of the room, use the next five minutes or so to calm down, offer a brief prayer asking God
for wisdom, and ask yourself what you need to say or
do when you go back to your spouse to refocus the
conversation. Returning with a new possible solution
or with a statement that reassures your spouse that you
really are on their side is always a good place to start if
you are stuck.

As for those "breaks" that occur at an 8 or higher,
they aren't breaks so much as breakdowns. If your conversation gets to an 8 or higher, it is best to stop the
discussion altogether, go to your separate corners for

several hours if possible, pray, and then return once you are calm enough to discuss the new possible solutions you've identified while you were apart.

6. Always Return to the Scene of the Crime

This habit is really important because, having allowed an argument to get over an 8, many couples would rather let things blow over and then pretend nothing ever happened. These spouses can be savagely attacking each other and then several hours later start chatting about what's for dinner. Although all seems normal on the outside, chances are the couple's blood pressure and stress-hormone levels are still quite high. Nothing has been resolved. They're just not going to talk about it.

The problem with this is that couples who do this never learn from their mistakes. They just pretend that whatever they argued about is never going to come up again, until it does, and then they're just as surprised as ever. Never underestimate your ability to be surprised by the same damn thing happening all over again.

The only way to defeat "deja vu all over again" syndrome is to intentionally return to the discussion when you are both calm again. But when you do, don't lead with more emotions. Instead, say something such as, "Listen, I was really upset when you did X, but that didn't give me the right to say (do) Y. I was thinking, if I had to do it over again, I might like to handle it Z. Would that be better for you?"

Feel free to use your own words as long as, when you return to the discussion, you are not revisiting who did what to whom and how angry you are about it. As we said before, your feelings are God's gift to you, not your spouse. Use your feelings to motivate you to identify the problem, seek God's wisdom, and then propose some possible solutions. If you can't think of what to do, tell your spouse that you'd like to sit down together and figure something out. Or seek professional assistance—especially if returning to a discussion consistently results in your just having the same argument again and again.

7. Did We Mention Prayer?

Finally, have we mentioned the importance of praying both individually and as a couple before, during, and after an argument? We have? Good. Let's mention it one more time then.

We're being a little facetious here to make the point that marriage truly is hard work, and there will be times that the only way you find the strength to go back in there one more time and try to work things out is because God won't stop bugging you to do it. You can ignore God and your spouse and your problems, but you do so at your peril. Please, for your sake, take time to pray before you sit down to discuss a serious issue. Say something such as, "God, please help us to be open to hearing each other's concerns and even more open to your will. Hail Mary . . ."

Then, when things start to heat up, pray again. Ask your spouse to pray with you. A good start might be, "Lord, this is really hard. We're sorry we're being so irritable and angry. Please help us get this back on track. Show us what you want us to do to solve this." If your spouse won't pray with you, then say the same prayer yourself when you employ the "take a break" technique we identified above.

Finally, after the argument, pray again. For instance, say, "God, thank you for helping us through this. It was really hard, but help us to learn from this. Help us to follow through with what we need to do next, and help us to heal any hurts we've caused each other. Thank you for your mercy and love. Help us to be more merciful and loving to each other every day."

Remember, the couple that prays together, stays together. Be that couple.

8. Finish the Discussion

This ought to go without saying, but we find it still needs to be said. If you finish an argument but you haven't identified any concrete action steps for what you need to do next to prevent similar problems from occurring in the future, then you haven't finished the discussion!

Most people really think that if they have vented their spleen, their job is done. Arguing is not about venting. That should be done on your own, or with God, or if you do it with your spouse, then do it with the understanding that you know that everything you are about to say is absolutely insane—but you just need to talk it out, and your spouse shouldn't take any of it personally, because it's just your feelings, and they're all a little nuts, and you get that. Problem solving begins after the venting is over. Make sure that you have identified action items, who is going to do what, and when exactly it's going to be done by. Otherwise, you haven't accomplished anything by your discussion, and you are going to be revisiting all this garbage sometime very soon. Save yourself the headache. Take an extra twenty minutes and make a plan.

We hope that the habits and suggestions we've made throughout this chapter will help give you the boost you need to get over the hurdles of the Conflict and Negotiation Stage. If you feel a little overwhelmed, that's okay. Take some time to let the information settle, and then read this chapter again, preferably with your spouse, and identify a handful of healthy problem solving habits you would like to cultivate in your marriage. Learning good problem-solving skills can be like learning the steps of a new dance. It can seem a little artificial and even forced at first. But the more you practice, the more graceful and second nature those new steps become. Your willingness to learn and apply new, more effective communication habits in the first few years of your marriage is what will help you respectfully negotiate your differences and help get you one step closer to becoming marriage masters as you build your lives and future together.

CHAPTER SIX

Marriage
Enemy #1

We do a fair number of radio and television interviews, as well as a great deal of public speaking at various marriage and family conferences around the world. In any of these contexts, one of the most popular questions put to us is, "What is the biggest reason marriages fall apart?"

Most people expect us to give answers such as "infidelity" or "addictions" or even "in-law problems," but the real answer is none of these. In fact, the most common reason for marital break-ups actually cause all of these problems and more.

The biggest contributor to marital problems and, eventually, marital breakdown is that husbands and wives tend to love their own comfort zones more than they love each other. This leads to no end of opportunities to feel rejected, resentful, and angry.

Back in chapter 2, we alluded to this problem when we talked about the fear of "losing themselves" that many couples experience in the Conflict and Negotiation Stage. Throughout marriage, but especially in the earlier years, husbands and wives are subjected to a dizzying number of changes: changes in their routines, challenges to their preferred ways of being and doing things, changes in their priorities, requests to change to accommodate each other, and more. It is easy to feel threatened by all this change, especially when it is your spouse who is asking you to change something about yourself. In the middle of all these opportunities for change, it can be extremely tempting to wrap your comfort zone around you as a baby blanket and, instead of responding positively to the call to change and grow, stubbornly refuse to give in.

"Comfort Zone" Defined

Some people ask us what we mean when we talk about "comfort zones." Your comfort zone represents the range of experiences, relationships, and ways of being that are familiar, common, and preferred. A comfort zone represents the way you like to live your life, dress, behave, and organize your day. Your comfort zone includes those things you know how to do well and things you enjoy doing in your free time—for instance, your hobbies, interests, and skills. It represents the way you prefer to act around people. For example, are you the life of the party, or do you like to keep to yourself? Likewise, your comfort zone represents the ways (and the degree to which) you like to give and receive affection. For example, do you like to display a lot of affection, or are you more reserved? Do you like exploring lots of different ways to show your love for each other (in and out of the bedroom), or are there certain things that are more comfortable and meaningful than others? In short, your comfort zone represents most of the preferences you may tend to think makes you "you."

The fact that marriage is a sacrament means, at least in part, that marriage is all about getting you and your spouse out of your comfort zones in order to create a unified couple. Why? Well, in a sense, a sacrament is a powerful engine that God uses to drive us toward sainthood, and as wonderful an idea as sainthood may be, there isn't a lot that's comfortable about it. People who are striving for sainthood (that is, anyone who considers himself or herself a Christian) must be willing to grow, to stretch, to be transformed from who they are today into the person God created them to be. We do that through the heroic generosity Catholics call "self-donation." That is the commitment to use everything we have—our time, talent, treasure, and even our bodies—to work for the good of others. This can sound like an intimidating call, a call meant, perhaps, for some special people

> The fact that marriage is a sacrament means, at least in part, that marriage is all about getting you and your spouse out of your comfort zones in order to create a unified couple.

but not for us. But it isn't just monks and missionaries and martyrs in far-off lands who are called to be saints. Every Catholic is called to strive for sainthood, and with God's grace, every Catholic can achieve it. As St. Thérèse of Lisieux showed us in her *Story of a Soul*, the path to sainthood doesn't necessitate great feats of derring-do. It just requires us to spend every moment of every day doing "small things with great love." If that isn't a recipe for a terrific marriage, we don't know what is.

Lovestyles

Among the biggest challenges to a couple's comfort zones—aside from the situations we discussed in chapter 2—are conflicts between a couple's "lovestyles." Lovestyles are the sensory-based ways individual men and women prefer to give or receive love. There are three lovestyles—visual, auditory, and kinesthetic—and each is based on the primary senses of sight, sound, and touch, respectively.

What we are referring to as lovestyles actually begin in childhood as learning styles. Every child learns differently, and their learning style is dependent on the sense that is most acutely developed in them. For instance, visual learners learn best by seeing notes on the board, looking at worksheets, viewing colorful bulletin boards, and other instructional methods that engage their sense of sight.

Auditory learners learn best through classroom discussions, verbal instruction, singing songs ("A, B, C, D, E, F, G . . .") and reciting poems ("Thirty days hath

September . . .), and other instructional methods that engage their sense of hearing.

Kinesthetic learners learn best by doing things. They learn best by using "manipulatives" (counting blocks, spelling with 3D letters), doing projects, playing games, and any other instructional method that engages their sense of touch.

To the degree that we all have senses of sight, hearing, and touch (smell and taste are also important in general, but less so for learning and communication), everyone does learn in all of these ways, but the way you learn best will depend on which of these senses tends to be most well developed in you.

As we mature, learning styles evolve into communication styles and, in relationship, loving styles, as they become the primary ways we like to give and receive affection and, in a sense, "learn" that the person we are in love with loves us back.

People with visual lovestyles need to "see" that you love them. In a sense, they feel love through their eyes. Tangible tokens of affection such as cards, flowers, notes, and little gifts mean the world to them because they can see the thought that went into them. People with a visual lovestyle feel that beauty is important. Dressing attractively is important. Setting the table nicely is important. Keeping the home neat and orderly is important. When they're stressed, people with a visual lovestyle tend to need to clean and straighten up their environment, since visual clutter just adds to the tension they are already feeling. Visual people like to make plans because they hate seeing blank spaces in the visual calendar they keep in their heads. Not having a plan stresses them out. When they want to be romantic, people with a visual lovestyle tend to prefer romantic lighting (candles, low light), neat, attractive spaces, and attractive clothing (whether dressing up to go out or wearing lingerie when having intimate time). People with a visual lovestyle need to "see" that you love them in order to truly feel loved.

By contrast, people with an auditory lovestyle "feel" love through their ears. They love to have long conversations about anything. They love hearing and saying "I love you" a million times a day. They love when you call them just to say, "I love you" or, "I was thinking about you." They have favorite songs that remind them of how much you love each other. They talk about feelings and want to hear you talk about your feelings too so that they can feel connected to you. They are very sensitive to tones of voice and will often detect slight differences in pitch and tone that make them aware of the other person being stressed or upset before the other person may even be aware of it. When people with an auditory lovestyle are stressed, they need to talk it out. They just want to be heard. They may not need you to solve the problem. They just need to hear themselves "doing the math" of solving the problem out loud. When they are feeling romantic, people with an auditory lovestyle love to tell you what they are feeling and why. They love pillow talk and maybe even telling romantic or erotic stories when they are being intimate. People with an auditory lovestyle need to hear you tell them how much you love them in the various words you use, sounds you make, and tones of voice you employ.

Finally, people with a kinesthetic (touch-oriented) lovestyle need to feel how much you love them through affection and acts of service. They tend to feel things very deeply but tend not to talk about their feelings. Instead they act on them. People with a kinesthetic lovestyle can have a hard time shifting out of whatever they are feeling in the moment and tend to think that whatever they are feeling now will last forever—until those feelings change, at which time, those feelings will last forever. They tend not to be very fussy about showing their love, preferring to do little things to take care of the person they care about or being physically affectionate. Just "being there" is very important to people with a kinesthetic lovestyle. Sometimes they feel most loved just sitting in a room with the person they care for and saying nothing for hours. They enjoy the comfort of not having to think of something to say and just being able to relax around somebody. If you ask a kinesthetic person if he or she loves you, he or she might say, "Of course! I wouldn't *be here* if I didn't!" (again, because just "being there" is a really important sign of love for the kinesthetic person). When they are stressed, people with a kinesthetic lovestyle will either tend to shut down and cocoon (take a nap, vegetate in front of the TV or computer, or just cuddle with the person they know cares most about them), or they will need to get the energy out by exercising or working on a project. When they are feeling romantic, the kinesthetic person will want to be physically affectionate—even if it seems to come out of the blue to his or her partner. They tend to like to not make a fuss about things— preferring that life and love be on a more even keel exactly because feelings affect them so much. They feel most loved when things "just happen." People with a kinesthetic lovestyle tend to be great at taking things easy and being present in the moment. They often hate to make plans because they don't know how they will feel by the time those plans will come around.

Obviously there is a lot of opportunity for confusion when two spouses have different lovestyles. This is a very common problem. Usually, a husband and wife will share at least some of one lovestyle but have secondary lovestyles that are different. This tends to be a problem when the couple gets stressed, because under stress, we all retreat to our preferred lovestyles and become more or less unable to attend to anything coming at us via another lovestyle. This can often manifest itself in marriage when a husband or wife will say, "I know my spouse loves me. I just don't feel it." In other words, I notice my spouse doing loving things, but they just aren't the things I need them to do in order to feel their love for me.

Discovering and accommodating to each other's lovestyles is an important challenge for all couples, but especially couples who are newly married. Because our lovestyles are neurologically based on our most well-developed senses, it can seem, nonsensical to love your spouse in ways that are different than the ways that naturally make sense to you. The kinesthetic spouse will feel in his or her bones that talking about his or her feelings is just stupid. It makes no sense that his or her auditory spouse needs to do this. The visual spouse will be offended when you don't put the card he or she brought home on the mantel where everyone can see how much he or she loves you.

The auditory spouse can't imagine why anyone wouldn't want to talk about everything all the time. It, literally, makes no sense!

In these cases, learning to love your spouse more than you love your comfort zone means being willing to be loving to your spouse in ways that make absolutely no sense to you but mean everything to your mate. At first, this will feel very difficult. With time, however, two things will happen. First, your marriage will get better because you will not only know that you love each other, but you will come to feel it in your bones. Second, you will actually become a better, more well-rounded person because you will develop those aspects of yourself—those senses—that to this point have been underdeveloped.

That's going to open up whole new worlds for you. Visual people who become more kinesthetic can (finally) learn to relax. Kinesthetic people who develop their auditory capacity can begin to talk about their feelings and change them instead of just feeling them. Auditory people who become more visual are better at making plans to solve problems instead of just talking about them. God gives you the spouse you need to grow in ways you'd never grow if you were left to

> Learning to love your spouse more than you love your comfort zone means being willing to be loving to your spouse in ways that make absolutely no sense to you but mean everything to your mate.

your own devices. The differences your spouse exhibits are really an invitation from God to you to grow in ways you need to grow in so that you can be the person he ultimately created you to be. Nothing good ever comes from refusing an invitation from God.

In a moment, we'll share some tips for stepping out of your comfort zone to learn to accommodate your spouse's lovestyle, but first, we'd like to share our experience of wrestling with this challenge.

⊙UR STORY

In the early years of our marriage, we were often challenged to be willing to leave our comfort zones for the sake of the other. (Of course, we still are, but it gets at least a little easier with practice.)

Greg says: For instance, when we were first married, we were great at telling each other we loved each other all the time, having long talks about anything, sharing our feelings, and having terrific conversations. These things (which, together, are called an "auditory lovestyle") were important ways that we helped each other feel loved and stay connected to one another.

But there were other things we needed from each other in order to feel safe, secure, and loved that did not come as naturally to us. For instance, Lisa likes quiet afternoons and evenings in which we can just hang out and be cozy—just get into sweats or something else comfortable and sit by the fire and read and cuddle and just "be" together. She tends not to like to plan too much for days off, preferring to just see what she feels like doing. (Incidentally, all of these things are consistent with a more kinesthetic lovestyle.)

Lisa says: These things made Greg twitch. He's always got a million projects going on in his head. He loves staying busy, and he always sees things that have to be done or would be great to do. He likes making plans and schedules, and he likes "doing things up." For instance, having a nice meal is fine, but it's even better if it's served on the nice dishes and the candles are lit. Cuddling is nice, but if the room we're cuddling in isn't basically neat, he has a hard time relaxing because he sees all the things that have to be done (and all of this is evident of the visual lovestyle).

Greg says: Of course, that made me seem incredibly fussy and impossible to please to Lisa. And honestly, I had a hard time thinking that Lisa wasn't just being lazy and unsupportive. Both of us would regularly get frustrated with the other, even though we were both trying to be as loving as we could to each other.

Lisa says: Exactly. Greg would bring home cards or flowers to show me how much he loved me. But I'd feel disappointed. After all, anyone could buy a card for someone. I just wanted Greg to stop running around doing things all the time and just "be" with me. But when I would just want to hang out and relax together, Greg felt like I was just expecting him to do everything while I hung out. When we would take time to be intimate, he would want to make the room look nice and light candles and maybe wear nice pajamas or lingerie to show each other how special this time was, and I'd feel hurt that I—all by myself, without all the fuss—wasn't enough. We both were working very hard to demonstrate our love for the other in ways that, literally, made sense to each of us but no sense at all to the other. We were working really hard, but we both still managed to feel a little lonely in spite of all the effort.

Greg says: Once we learned about our different lovestyles, we were able to understand that the other person wasn't an idiot. We just sensed our love for each other in different ways. If I wanted Lisa to feel how much I loved her, I had to make myself stop being so busy all the time and learn to sit still and just hold her and be quiet together.

Lisa says: And if I wanted Greg to feel how much I loved him, I had to get used to the idea that dressing nicely in or out of the bedroom, or taking some time to make the room look nice, or finding other ways to show (instead of just telling or feeling) my love for him didn't mean I wasn't enough.

Greg says: It wasn't easy, but it was definitely worth it. We developed a simple exercise to help us remember the kinds of things that made each other feel loved, and we came up with ways that helped us remember to do those things so that we could support each other while we were learning. In time, a funny thing happened. Certainly, our marriage became more warm and loving. We both felt closer to the other as we saw how hard the other was trying to accommodate our own lovestyle, but on top of that, we both began to grow as persons. Now, Lisa has developed her visual capacities. She has become a terrific decorator, has a great fashion sense, and likes to keep things neat and orderly to keep her stress down.

Lisa says: Over the years, Greg has developed his kinesthetic side, and he has learned to relax. He still enjoys doing things, but he doesn't feel as if he always has to be doing something. He can let the crooked picture frame be if he has a choice between straightening it and sitting with me and just taking some time to hang out together. We've kept all the best parts of what we were, but we've helped each other develop new dimensions of our personalities as well. By opening ourselves to each other's lovestyles, we've learned to be more well-rounded, more developed people in our own right, and we each have the other to thank for it.

Greg says: Another unexpected fruit of this work to leave our comfort zones behind and accommodate each other's lovestyles is that we have experienced spiritual benefits as well. It makes sense, of course, because God calls to us through our senses. Spirituality is a sensual call (by God) that leads to a transformative response (in us). The more we develop our capacity to relate to each other and the world through all of our senses, the more ways we give God to reach out to us. By developing my kinesthetic side, I've been able to become a more compassionate and contemplative person. I've gotten better at listening to God in the silence I've been able to carve out, a silence I found difficult to tolerate in my more purely visual days.

Lisa says: And I've become more joyful because I'm able to encounter God more directly through beauty and order. I was always able to experience God in these ways to some degree in the past, but my work to develop my visual self has really helped me take this to a new level. It's been exciting to find God reaching out in these new ways.

As we shared earlier in this book, the Church teaches us that we find ourselves by making a sincere gift of ourselves. By working to leave our comfort zones for the sake of making a more perfect gift of ourselves to each other, we discovered with God's help new dimensions of ourselves, opened up new doors to intimacy in our marriage, and touched our souls in ways we couldn't have dreamed of had we not accepted his invitation to grow for the sake of each other.

Imagine what God can do for you if you accept his invitation to leave your comfort zones behind and grow for the sake of your beloved.

We discuss lovestyles more extensively in our book *For Better . . . Forever!: A Catholic Guide to Lifelong Marriage.*[17] In that book, we include checklists and quizzes to help you and your spouse learn your respective lovestyles, and we suggest ways that you can expand your capacity for expressing love for your partner through all three lovestyles. That said, our shorter discussion here can be enough to get you started down the path.

Lovelist Exercise

As you read when we shared our story, we have developed this simple exercise to make it easier for couples to discover and attend to each other's lovestyles.

Step One: Make Your List

Take some time for both you and your spouse to write down at least twenty-five things that make you, personally, feel loved when your spouse does them for you. These could be things that your spouse currently does, things you wish they would do more of, or things that you would like them to start doing. Identify at least twenty-five things that make you feel loved on a gut level; that is, write down those things that, when your spouse does them, make you think, "That was really sweet/thoughtful/kind! (S)he didn't have to do that!" Try to think of things your spouse does—or could do—to make your average day a little easier or more pleasant.

This always seems easier to do than it is, and most couples get stuck after the first few ideas. Here are a few tips to generate some additional ideas.

1. Be specific and concrete. Don't just write, "Be more affectionate." List all the ways that your spouse could be meaningfully affectionate to you. For instance, "Make sure you give me a hug before your leave for work." "Hold my hand when we are walking together." "Kiss my neck." "Ask if you can give me a back rub." See? One big, vague idea suddenly becomes four specific, concrete ideas. To generate a bigger list (giving your spouse more ideas means giving them more ways to love you) look at each item and see if you could break it down into more specific and concrete examples.

2. Be positive. This is not a complaint list. Don't write, "I'll feel loved when you start picking up your damn socks!" You could write, "I feel loved when you help me keep the house neat without my asking." The point is, this is a Lovelist, not a complaint list. Tell your spouse what they can do for you, not what you wish they'd stop doing.

3. Keep it simple. Try not to list things that take significant amounts of time, effort, or money. This
   list isn't so much about vacations or weekends
   away or fancy dinners out as it is about little,
   thoughtful things that you can do to make each
   other's days easier and more pleasant. "I love
   when you bring home my favorite ice cream,"
   "I love when you call me to ask how my day is
   going," "I feel loved when you smile at me when
   you see me," and "I feel loved when you initiate lovemaking" are all examples of the kinds of
   simple gestures that mean a lot.

STEP TWO: TRADE AND DISCUSS

Once you each have at least twenty-five items on
your list, trade them and discuss any questions you
have about the items your partner has identified.
Chances are you won't be too surprised by many
of the things on your spouse's list, but there may
be a few things that you weren't expecting, and
there may even be a few things that make you a
little uncomfortable. By all means, you should feel
free to ask questions about anything your spouse
wrote that you don't completely understand, but
resist the urge to react negatively to your spouse's
list. Remember, by opening up your hearts to each
other and telling each other what you need, you
have made yourselves vulnerable to each other.
Be sensitive to that.

> We find ourselves by making a gift of ourselves.

Remember also that
we find ourselves by making a gift of ourselves.

Assuming that your spouse has not written anything that is objectively immoral or demeaning, be
generous. Recall that the needs and desires written
on your mate's heart are an invitation from God to
you to grow in ways that would never occur to you
if God hadn't called you together. Accept this invitation from God to leave your comfort zone for the
sake of love—for the sake of learning to be a better
gift to each other.

STEP THREE: LIVE THE LIST

Each day, look at your spouse's Lovelist in the morning. Think of opportunities you might have in your
day to do the things on the list. Don't assume you'll
get to it. Make a plan, and be intentional about it.
Make a commitment to do at least two things on
the list that come more easily to you plus one thing
that is a bit of a stretch. Some days this will be easier
than others. That's okay. The point is that you are
making a consistent effort to open your hearts and
minds more and more to each other over time.

Also, you don't have to just "stick to the script,"
as it were. Use the items on the list as an inspiration.
Feel free to do things that aren't on your spouse's
list, but seem similar to things he or she has written down. If you do this, keep two things in mind.
First, don't substitute things that would be more
comfortable for you. Try to generate new ideas that
offer the same level of challenge to your comfort
zone as the items that inspired those new ideas.
Challenging each other to grow is, after all, one of
the major points of this exercise. Second, be sure to

discuss these new efforts with your spouse to make sure you're hitting the mark.

STEP FOUR: DISCUSS DAILY

This step is almost more important than making the list itself. In order to prevent the Lovelist from being something you write and then promptly forget about, there has to be some kind of regular follow-up. Take some time over dinner, or at the end of each day, to talk about the things you tried to do for each other that day. This is neither a time for score keeping nor criticizing. Resist the urge to grade each other's effort or treat this as some kind of competition demonstrating who loves whom more.

Instead, view this as a time to acknowledge each other's sincere efforts to be more loving. If you like, you can use the following talking points to guide your discussion.

Share your efforts. Each of you should take a moment to share some of the things you tried to do for each other that day. Don't just list what you did. Explain why you thought those items would be meaningful to your spouse. For example, "I knew you were having a stressful day, and I know that it usually helps you relax when I rub your shoulders. That's why I told you this morning that I'd like to take some time this evening to give you a massage." Or, "I knew we haven't had a lot of time together lately, so I wanted to be sure to make at least a little connection with you during the day.

That's why I called from work between my meetings just to say, 'I love you.'"

Acknowledge each other's efforts. You don't have to give a medal or throw a parade for each other, but take a moment to thank each other for what you did and explain why it was meaningful. For example, "You know, I really did appreciate that call. I know how busy you were today, and it meant a lot to know that you were thinking about me in the middle of all that craziness at the office. Thank you."

This would also be a good time to mention any things your partner did that you appreciated but he or she didn't mention. For example, "I know it's not on my list, but it really meant a lot to me when I went to unload the dishwasher and I saw that you already did it. That was a nice break." Doing this gives you an opportunity to both acknowledge each other's extra little efforts and possibly give you new items to add to your list.

Ask how you might serve each other tomorrow. This is your chance to plan ahead. Ask your spouse to tell you a little bit about his or her day tomorrow. As you listen, think about items on the list—and other ideas—that would help you make your spouse's day a little easier or more pleasant. For example, "Hey, you mentioned that you were worried about that meeting tomorrow. Would you like me to call you sometime before the meeting so that we could pray about it together?" Or, "It sounds as if you have a lot of errands to run. I'm going past the dry cleaner's tomorrow. I'd be happy to pick up your dress."

If you can't think of any ideas for making your partner's day a little easier or more pleasant, ask your spouse what he or she might like you to do. You don't have to just do those specific things, but it will give you a starting point. Sometimes, neither of you will have any ideas. That can be okay, too, assuming that you're both taking the effort seriously. Sometimes, it's enough to know that your spouse cares enough to ask if he or she can help. Many days, knowing that you aren't alone is the best gift you can give each other. Regardless, make sure that you still use the list the next day to find little ways to care for each other and stretch your capacity for love.

Choosing Love

In the first few years of marriage, one of the biggest challenges is the temptation to cling to what's familiar and comfortable out of a fear of "losing yourself" in the relationship. But the truth is we find ourselves—and everything God created us to be—when we step outside our comfort zones for the sake of loving our spouse. Negotiating lovestyles and being willing to create new patterns that substitute for old preferences are two ways we've invited you to leave behind your comfort zones for the sake of a better marriage and personal growth. No doubt you will experience many other times when you will be asked to choose love over comfort. Embracing this choice in the early years of your marriage by choosing to love to each other more than you love your own comfort zones will set you and your spouse on the road to becoming marriage masters. Even more so, the good choices you make in the first five years will guarantee that God will be able to use your marriage to show the world all the wonderful things he can do in the lives of those who choose love first at every stage of married life.

CHAPTER SEVEN

First Comes Marriage

In this chapter we will be examining specific traits and tools that characterize and help a marriage get off on the right foot from the beginning. We recommend getting a pen and writing pad or journal ready, since you will be prompted to create lists and goals for you and your spouse.

Elisa is frustrated with the amount of time she and her husband, Mario, spend with his family. "It isn't that I don't like them. It's just that we're over there all the time. I don't feel as if we're able to make time for each other. Eventually we're going to have our own children, and I want to be our own family, not just an extension of his."

For his part, Mario is frustrated with what he sees as a lack of generosity on Elisa's part. "My family has always been tight. I just wish Ellie could be happy that my family loves her and wants to include us. I don't understand why this is such a thing for her."

∞

Alan and Rebecca regularly argue over her work schedule. "I just wish Alan could be more supportive of my career. We've talked about my cutting back on my hours when we have kids, and I'm okay with that. But I feel as if that puts a lot of pressure on me now to achieve a certain level at work because my progress there is going to be stalled when we start our family. I don't understand what he doesn't get about that."

Alan says, "I completely support Rebecca's desire to do well in her work. One of the things I love about her is her motivation and drive. I think that's awesome. I just don't understand why she has to sacrifice everything else for work. She's never home when she says she's going to be. We're not able to go on dates consistently, and I just feel as if there isn't time to be a couple, much less even start thinking about starting a family. I don't want to be in Rebecca's way. I just wish she valued our marriage a little more."

∞

Most couples know that marriage requires fidelity, but what you may not know is that fidelity means more than refusing to have other romantic or sexual partners. Because marriage is your vocation—that is, the primary way you will work out your baptismal mission, become what you were created to be in this life, and help each other get to heaven in the next—there is no other relationship or activity that could be more important than your marriage and family life. That doesn't mean that you aren't allowed to have other friendships, or a great relationship with your mom or dad, or compelling and interesting work and hobbies, but it does mean that your marriage has to get the best of your time and energy, not just what's left of it after you're done with everyone and everything else.

This idea is terrifically countercultural. Most people think of a marriage or family as something they have (like any other possession or acquisition), but it's much more than that. It is important to think of marriage as an actual activity, an activity that requires time, energy, and practice to become good at. If you wanted to be good at golf, you wouldn't just buy a set of clubs and then leave it in the closet. You'd make time to go to the golf course and practice. If you want to be good at your career, you make time to get your work done and get regular training on how to do an even better job. You see these things as activities, and so you work at them.

But as we say, most couples think of marriage as a possession. On the day we say, "I do," we get our marriage certificate—our diploma to adulthood—and that's that. Mission accomplished. Now we can get on with other achievements. Marriage becomes just one more item on the bucket list to check off, or one more certificate to hang on the wall. True, most couples

In the broadest sense of the word, fidelity represents your ability to put your marriage first while still prioritizing the other important work and relationships in your life.

don't intentionally and consciously think of marriage this way, but most couples do treat their marriage this way. They tend to take their relationship for granted, and they can tend to become resentful when taking care of it encroaches on other important work and relationships. In fact, the hesitation, frustration, or resentment you may feel when your spouse asks for more time or energy for them or the marriage is often the best indicator of an unconscious tendency to view marriage as a thing instead of the most important activity of your live. Resolving this tension is the work of fidelity.

The truth is every couple struggles to find the right balance here. In the broadest sense of the word, fidelity represents your ability to put your marriage first while still prioritizing the other important work and relationships in your life. This chapter will give you two habits you can practice, especially in the earlier years of your life together, that will help you achieve and maintain that balance both now and for years to come.

What Does Your Marriage Run On?

Most cars require gasoline to run. Some cars use more gas than others, and the amount they use represents their "fuel economy." When you buy a car you have to respect whatever fuel economy it gets. For instance, if your car got twenty miles a gallon and your tank held fifteen gallons, you'd have to gas it up every three hundred miles whether you wanted to or not (whew—we now conclude the math portion of our book). It's just what your car needs. No amount of complaining, criticizing, or resenting the car will make it give you better mileage. Refueling every three hundred miles is just what you need to do to prevent your car from running out of gas and leaving you stranded and cursing on the side of the road. You like the car. You bought the car. So you accept and respect what it needs you to do so that it can get you from point A to point B.

In the same way all relationships, especially marriage and family relationships, run on time. Some marriages require more time than others, and when you choose to be in a relationship, you have to respect the "time economy" that relationship gets—metaphorically speaking. If your marriage requires X amount of time to run well, that's just what it takes. You like your spouse. You picked your spouse. So now you have to respect the amount of time that person requires from you to be sure of you. It doesn't matter that your family of origin didn't use that much time to function well. It doesn't matter that this friendship or that requires significantly less time than your spouse does to feel secure with you. Those are different "cars," and they have different "fuel economy." You have to respect your marriage for the unique relationship it is. If you don't want your marriage to break down and leave you stranded and cursing on the side of the road, you need to make sure that you are giving it the fuel—the time—it requires to get

you from now to "'til death do us part." Cultivating
the following two habits can help you respect the time
economy your marriage requires while still leaving you
time and energy to do interesting work and care for the
other important people in your life.

I. Conscious Prioritizing

Most people tend to be fairly unconscious about the
way they prioritize their life. Our boss asks us to do
certain things, our families of origin ask us to do certain
things, our friends ask us to do certain things, and our
hearts want us to pursue still other things. We say yes
to all those requests, and that constitutes our schedule
for the week. Whatever's left is what we give to our
marriage. While this habit is entirely well intended, it
spells disaster if practiced in any relationship, especially
marriage and family life.

Some relationships are worth protecting. Our promise of fidelity on the day we said, "I do," means that
we recognize that our marriage is one relationship that
is deserving of that protection. The first habit couples
need to cultivate in order to be able to give the time and
energy they need to give to their marriage while still
having time for other important people and commitments is Conscious Prioritizing. The following exercise
will help you organize your time and priorities more
effectively.

Conscious Prioritizing Exercise

How much time does your marriage need to function well? Believe it or not, it is possible to come up with a ballpark number of hours per week you need to invest in your marriage to properly maintain it. Here's how you do it. First, think of the things you and your spouse do together in an average week. Write down those things (i.e., dinner, prayer time, time for working on projects together, dates, etc.) in the blanks below and estimate the amount of time those activities take (i.e., fifteen minutes, an hour, two hours). Note, this is not an ideal list or a list of the way you wish things were. This is a list of what you actually do now and how much time it takes to do those things. List these times together, and tally up the amount of time you spend together in an average week.

Activity	Estimated Amount of Time
_____	_____
_____	_____
_____	_____
_____	_____
_____	_____

Average Amount of Time Together

_____

Now, think of another week (still a regular week, not vacation time) when, for whatever reason, you and your spouse felt as if you were doing better than normal—a week in which you and your husband or wife felt a little more close and connected than usual. Now, ask yourself, "What did we do together that week that we usually don't make time for?" Write down those activities in the blanks below, estimate the amount of time those activities took, and tally up the amount.

Activity   **Estimated Amount of Time**

_____   _____

_____   _____

_____   _____

_____   _____

_____   _____

Extra Amount of Time Together to Feel "Special"

_____

Next, add up the two totals (average amount of time + extra "special" time) and write the number below.

(Average Amount of Time _____) +

(Extra "Special" Time Together _____) =

_____ (Time Economy)

The average amount of time you spend together added to the extra time you invest in your relationship when you feel a little closer than usual represents your "time economy"—the amount of time your relationship needs you to give it each week in order to function at its best and for the two of you to feel as close to each other as you are meant to normally feel.

Sometimes, a husband or wife might need a little less time than his or her spouse to feel close. That's beside the point. Remember, the number we're looking for is the amount of time it takes for both of you to feel satisfied with the relationship, not just one of you.

In order to give your relationship the energy it deserves, you'll need to start working toward intentionally carving out this amount of time every week for each other. Of course, the actual amount of time you spend on your relationship may vary a bit from week to week, and, of course, some weeks you may need to travel for work, or your kids might be sick, or other unusual things might come up that prevent you from giving this time to your relationship. As long as these interruptions are the exception and not the rule, you should be just fine. You shouldn't feel as if you have to be a slave to the time economy number you came up with. It is there to be a rule of thumb that can help you and your spouse get a more concrete sense of how much time you need to devote to the "activity" of marriage in order to feel as if you're doing it well.

One last point. If and when you have children, this exercise doesn't just have to refer to time when you and your spouse are alone. The lists can include time with your children that helps you and your spouse feel closer to each other. Family dinners, game nights, family days, and family prayer can all be important marriage builders, too. But if you include these activities on your "average week" list, be sure to add the little stolen moments together for work, prayer, play, and intimacy on your "special" activity list.

At the beginning of each week, we recommend sitting down with your planners and figuring out how you are going to be sure to carve out time for these and similar activities that help you maintain your marriage. In the very early days, this time tends to "just happen," but as your family grows and your commitments increase, practicing conscious prioritizing of your time will help prevent you and your spouse from growing apart—especially when you hit that busy Creative Stage of marriage (about seven to fifteen or more years) when kids and careers take off and a couple has to hold on to each other extra tight to keep from being pulled apart by all the demands placed on their time.

2. Rituals and Routines

The second habit couples need to commit to in the earlier years of marriage is the establishment and protection of regular rituals and routines.

Rituals refers to those regular, scheduled, and expected times a couple carves out for working, praying, playing, and loving together. The Conscious Prioritizing exercise helps you identify the kinds of activities that draw you together and helps you figure out how much time you need to lay aside to do them. Ritualizing those activities enables you to count on those activities happening consistently (instead of once in a blue moon when you happen to remember them) by getting them on the calendar at the same day and time every week (or any other regular interval, such as the same time every day, month, etc.). Turning an activity into a ritual means that you've come to count on it as a regular, important, and eagerly anticipated event in your life. "Oh, it's Tuesday! We have game night tonight!" "Hey, honey, it's almost eight o'clock. Will you be ready for our prayer time?" "I always look forward to Saturday mornings. I love having breakfast with you and working together on some household project." "The second Sunday of every month we go to brunch with our best friends."

Having regular rituals allows a couple to build a body of experiences and mini celebrations that serve as common points of reference. They enable you to grow closer because of all your shared moments. Surprisingly for most, living under the same roof and more or less being around each other all the time doesn't actually do anything to build a relationship. By contrast, intentionally having regular, shared experiences builds intimacy, creates a sense of belonging, and helps you do things closer couples do—finish each other's sentences. The more rituals you have, the better you know how each other thinks and works in a variety of circumstances and the closer you will feel to each other.

Routines, on the other hand, have to do with the regular, expected, and orderly ways you approach different tasks or different parts of your day. Routines are patterned habits that start out conscious and then quickly become unconscious. The way you get ready in the morning, bedtime routines, regular housework time, the process of setting the table for dinner or straightening up together before bed, and other more mundane but still regular and cooperative activities are all examples of routines. Routines help you know that you'll get your laundry done on Wednesdays, you'll have dinner at six o'clock each evening, you will always straighten up the bathroom before you will go to work, and you will go grocery shopping on Thursday evenings. If rituals build marital unity by creating moments, routines build marital harmony by creating safety and order. Routines help us know what to expect. They become the assumed "way that we, as a couple, do things."

Fifty years of research on the power of rituals and routines suggests that both are essential, not just for marriage and family harmony, but for the mental health and emotional well-being of the individual spouses.[18] Without rituals, there is no sense of "us." Without routines, everything is in chaos, since we have to reinvent how we do everything each time we do it.[19]

Rituals and routines tend to evolve spontaneously as a couple resolves the drama of the Conflict and Negotiation Stage we spoke of earlier in the book. But by being more intentional about them, couples can increase the power of their rituals and routines to draw them closer together and give them greater peace.

RITUAL AND ROUTINE EXERCISE

In the last exercise of this chapter, we'd like to give you an opportunity to strengthen the rituals and routines that bind you together and make you unique as a couple. In part I, you'll have an opportunity to look at or develop the routines you have that make sure you get the time you need to work, play, pray, communicate, and celebrate together. In part II, you'll look at or bring greater clarity to the routines that help manage your expectations of each other and bring order to your lives together.

PART I: RITUALS

A ritual is a regular, scheduled, expected event that enables you to have the time you need to work, play, pray, communicate, and celebrate together. Sit down with your spouse, and consider your relationship. In the blanks below, write the rituals that mean the most to you in the following categories: work, play, prayer, communication, and celebrations. If you don't have entries for a particular category, discuss rituals you could create to shore up this part of your lives together.

Work: Every week, we have regular, scheduled time to work together to keep our home and lives in good order. The following are some of the times and ways we work together that mean the most to us.

_____

_____

Play: Every week, we have regular, scheduled time to celebrate our lives together by doing something enjoyable that brings us closer. The following are some of the times and ways we play together that mean the most to us.

_____

_____

Prayer: Every day, and throughout the week, we have regular, scheduled times and to come together before God to thank him for his gifts and ask for his guidance and help. The following are some of the times and ways we pray together that mean the most to us.

_____

_____

Communication: Every day and throughout the week we make time to talk about our days, our schedules, and more important things such as the direction of our individual lives and our life as a couple. The following are some of the times and ways we make time for communication that mean the most to us.

_____

_____

Celebration: Throughout the year, on birthdays, anniversaries, special seasons, and holidays, we have traditions that we look forward to. The following are some of the traditions that mean the most to us.

Birthday Traditions: _____

_____

Anniversary Traditions: _____

_____

Seasonal Traditions (nonholiday traditions that happen every winter, spring, summer, or fall): _____

_____

Holiday Traditions: _____

_____

Other Important Rituals: Every couple has certain rituals that set them apart (e.g., unique celebrations, a special place they like to visit regularly, certain meaningful activities or experiences they regularly share together). The following are some of the unique rituals that make us "us."

_____

_____

PART II: ROUTINES

Routines bring order to the common, everyday events of your life. They represent the way you manage each other's expectations about chores, the way you spend your time, the way you organize your day, and the way you make decisions. In the blanks below, identify the routines that mean the most to you. If you don't have entries for a particular category, discuss routines you could create to shore up this part of your lives together.

Describe your morning routine. Does it work for you both? Are there ways you would like to adjust your routine so that things go more smoothly?

_____

_____

Describe the way you prepare your meals. Does it work for you both? Are there ways you would like to adjust your routine so that things go more smoothly?

_____

_____

Describe the way you do your regular chores (laundry, dishes, housekeeping, yard work, grocery shopping). Does it work for you both? Are there ways you would like to adjust your routine so that things go more smoothly?

_____

_____

Describe the time you have at home in the evening together (e.g., when you have dinner, how you clean up after, what you do after dinner, and how and when you get ready for bed). Does it work for you both? Are there ways you would like to adjust your routine so that things go more smoothly?

_____

_____

Conclusion

Throughout this chapter we've looked at ways you can always put each other and your marriage first. Too many couples take the early years together for granted, only to be surprised to find their relationship squeezed out once families start growing, careers take off, and life gets going at full steam. Establishing the habits we've discussed in this chapter—conscious prioritizing and establishing rituals and routines—will help make sure that you never grow apart and, better still, grow closer together as life picks up speed.

CHAPTER EIGHT

Money
Madness

Until now, we've been looking at your marriage as a
whole and identifying the attitudes and habits that can
help you set the stage for becoming marriage masters
in your early years together. In the next few chapters,
we'll take a closer look at some of the most common
issues that drive couples of any age or stage crazy—
topics such as money, in-laws, sex, and becoming new
parents. Let's start with some ideas for getting on the
same page about money.

What Does Money Mean to You?

We need to say up front that we are not financial planners. We will not be giving you financial advice per
se. But what every financial planner, accountant, or
investment consultant will tell you is that conflict about

money in marriage has little to do with the ins and outs about financial management and everything to do with how you and your spouse feel about money and what money means to you. For some, money means security. For others, money is for fun. And for still others, money is freedom, a nuisance, status, or something else entirely. In this chapter we'll help you discover what money means to you and help you move toward a Christian sensibility toward money management. We'll help you negotiate your spending and saving styles and give you some ideas for having constructive conversations about money and budgeting. At the end of the chapter we'll offer some additional resources for acquiring better money-management skills.

◯◯

Nick and Maria have a pretty great relationship, except when it comes to money. That's when the gloves come off.

"We have our worst fights around paying bills. Nick wants to get the bills done, but he'll write checks without writing down what he paid and to whom. Then I have no record of what's paid and what isn't. It makes me furious, because I see all these checks gone, I have no idea what they're for, and I don't know what's left in the account! Sure, I could check the balance online, but that doesn't tell me what payments might still be out there. And anyway, our accountant says that we should never just trust the online balance. We need our own records in case something goes wrong—such as identity theft or something. Nick acts as if I'm crazy when I bring any of this up.

For his part Nick says he just forgets. "I know I drive Maria crazy. I don't mean to, but I just forget about it. It stresses me out to think about money, so when I get busy or in a rush I just don't have the energy for it. We're never overdrawn. I don't know what the big deal is."

Maria rolls her eyes, "We're never overdrawn because I obsess over not letting it get overdrawn. It drives me crazy how thoughtless he is. It's the only thing he's thoughtless about, but it's a big thing!"

○○

Alejandro and Jenn don't do well when it comes to spending.

Alejandro says, "I just need Jenn to get control of her spending. She's constantly buying things whether we need them or not. Anytime I say something, she gets so defensive!"

Jenn responds, "He's such a tightwad! It isn't as if I'm some kind of shopping addict or something. I know what we have, and I always try to be careful. He just thinks that every penny we don't have to spend on food or necessary bills should go in the bank. I'm all for saving, but I'd like to be able to have some nice things, too. The other day, I came home with some new throw pillows for the couch. I got them on sale. It cost me all of thirty dollars. You would have thought

I sold his mother to pay off my gambling debts from the way he acted!"

"I just don't understand why we need new throw pillows! The old ones looked fine."

"And you didn't want those either. This summer, I want to take a little vacation. I'm getting a bonus at work, and I'd like to do something nice with it. Al doesn't think we should go anywhere. He just wants to stay home and sock it away in the bank. Again, I don't mind saving, but is it okay to want some kind of quality of life? No matter how much we save, he's always pushing to save more. It sounds admirable, until he starts nickel-and-diming every purchase I make. I never knew what a control freak he was until we started handling money together."

"It's not that at all! Why can't you just be happy with what you have for a change?" Alejandro retorts.

○○

The Meaning of Money

The reality is that all the financial know-how in the world probably isn't going to help the couples above. Obviously good information never hurt anyone, but the arguments we recounted have much more to do with what money means to these couples than it does with a lack of financial-management skills. Financial planners can give you skills, but they won't help Nick if he won't use them. Financial planners can give you advice to reach your goals, but Alejandro and Jenn can't agree on what those goals should be. Again, we're not saying that couples shouldn't seek competent financial guidance; it's just that most people ignore the emotional dimension of money management, and if you don't attend to that level of things, the best advice won't help you.

Regardless of what money means to you, any discussion about finances in a Christian household needs to begin with what the Church tells us about how God wants us to think about and handle money. For the most part, money is one of those areas where the faithful have wide latitude to handle it how we see fit, but there are a few principles that every Catholic should keep in mind.

Catholics and Money: First Principles

Scripture reminds us of the importance of avoiding both greed (Prv 23:4) and excessive debt (Prv 24:7). As far as our income goes, the *Catechism of the Catholic Church* tells us that we have a right to earn a "dignified livelihood" for ourselves and our families.[20] We also have the right to save money and own things (goods and property) that help us enjoy life as a gift from God[21] and even maintain a certain state in life.[22]

> We are stewards (caretakers) of what we have, not absolute masters.

That said, the catechism reminds us that everything we have is to be used to work for the good of people— first our families, and then others. We are stewards (caretakers) of what we have, not absolute masters. This is because, ultimately, everything we have belongs to God and is a gift from God. As such, he expects us to share his generosity with the people who need it—beginning with our family and then extending to others. We are also reminded that we must keep the virtues of temperance, justice, and solidarity in mind when deciding the appropriate ways to handle our finances.

In economic matters, respect for human dignity requires the practice of the virtue of temperance, so as to moderate attachment to this world's goods; the practice of the virtue of justice, to preserve our neighbor's rights and render him what is his due; and the practice of solidarity, in accordance with the golden rule and in keeping with the generosity of the Lord, who "though he was rich, yet for your sake . . . became poor so that by his poverty, you might become rich" (2 Cor 8:9).

In sum, it's perfectly fine for us to enjoy the gifts that God has given us, to purchase things that make our lives safer or more enjoyable, and to save money both for our basic security and for important milestones in life (a home, children's college education, retirement). At the same time, we must always remember two things:

1. Money and the things we own must always, always, always be at the service of the people in our lives (as opposed to the other way around).

2. We must do what we can with what we have to try to ease the burdens of others.

People (first our own family and then our neighbors) must always be our first concern when deciding how to manage our finances. How you do this in your family is ultimately your choice, but your decisions must be made in a spirit of prayer and a humble desire to do what God would want you to do with the gifts he has given you from his treasury.

Handling Money, Together

Now that we have a basic idea of how God asks us to approach our finances, let's look at how to apply those principles in your marriage and establish good money-management attitudes that will serve you for years to come.

1. Examine Your Conscience

At the beginning of the chapter, we mentioned that the most challenging thing about money isn't the practical skills but the emotional meaning behind it. Now is the time to look at what money means to you and how that squares with what God tells us is a healthy attitude toward money as revealed in our discussion above.

 MONEY AND MOTIVATION EXERCISE

Consider the following questions in light of our reflection above, and discuss your answers with each other.

a. Money can mean different things to different people: security, freedom, fun, independence, power, and so on. When it comes to money, are you happier when spending or saving? If spending, what do you like to spend the most on? If saving, what are you saving for? Why are those things important? When you have the answer to these questions, you will have a clearer sense

of what money means to you. Write down your
answers.

b. Consider your answers to the questions above.
Where did you learn to think about money this
way? What experiences in your childhood or life
before marriage formed your attitudes toward
money?

c. Now consider these motivations in light of our
discussion of the godly purpose of money and
goods. Chances are there are some good things
about the ways you think about money and some
possibilities for abuse. What do you think are the
strengths about the way you think about money,
and what do you think are the biggest tempta-
tions you need to avoid in light of the above
principles regarding Christians and finances?

d. Finally, if you have not yet done so, discuss your
answers to the previous questions with each
other. In what ways do you think you will need
to try to be more sensitive to your mate's feelings
about money? What specific things might each
of you do to be more considerate of the way
each of you thinks about money?

The questions above have three purposes.

First, it's important to get in touch with the thoughts
and feelings you have about money—and where you
learned to think that way—so that when you and your
spouse have financial conversations, you know what
you are really discussing. For instance, let's consider the
examples that began the chapter. What if Nick's financial irresponsibility was really an attempt not to be like

his dad, who was obsessed with money and so much of a workaholic that Nick never really got to know him? And what if Maria's mom was a single mom who only made it financially because she was so good at accounting for every penny? Likewise, it would be easy for Alejandro and Jenn to think they were arguing about whether they should take a nice vacation or not. But what if the conversation was really about Jenn's need to have a sense of family because her parents' divorce prevented her from ever having family vacations and the fond memories and sense of closeness that go with them? And what if Jenn's feelings were conflicting with the fact that Alejandro was always worried as a child because his dad had a chronic illness that affected his ability to work, and his mom was always going on about how they were going to lose the house if his dad didn't get better? Arguments about money are never as simple as they seem. Being aware of the experiences that formed each other's attitudes toward money will help you be sensitive to each other's real concerns so that you can be more compassionate to each other's needs and feelings.

Second, it's important to keep a close eye on our emotional baggage about money. Just because you came by your feelings about money for legitimate reasons doesn't mean your feelings are always healthy or right. Chances are your emotional history with money makes you good at some aspect of financial management but not so good at others. For instance, Jenn might be good at remembering that money exists to serve people, to create good family memories and experiences, and to create a warm and loving home, but she might not be as sensitive to the need to save for a rainy day. Alejandro might be great at saving, but he might not be as appreciative of the need to enjoy the life God has given him instead of just hoping that he can survive it another day. Being aware of each other's strengths and weaknesses when it comes to our attitudes about money helps couples know when to respect each other's expertise and how to balance our own biases.

Third, regardless of what our own experiences have taught us and what our own feelings are, we are always obliged to check how we naturally come at things against how God needs us to approach them. That's both so that God can heal what is broken in us and so that God can, as we shared earlier, change the world through your marriage and the gifts he's shared with you. There is no shame in recognizing that your heart isn't quite where it needs to be when it comes to God's plan for your finances, but recognizing that gives us the humility we need to be willing to learn from each other and allow God to work in us so that we might be better stewards in the world. We thought we'd share a little bit of our experience as a way of illustrating how this process has been a blessing to us over the years. Afterward, we'll offer some additional tips for establishing healthy money management.

OUR STORY

We both have very different backgrounds when
it comes to money, and it took a while for us to

figure out how to manage each other's styles respectfully.

Greg says: Growing up, my parents owned and operated their own photography studio. My dad loved photography, but he wasn't the best businessman. My mom wasn't really any better. As time went by, some of the poor business decisions they made caused an initially promising business to limp along for years. To their credit, the business supported our family as long as dad lived, but it was a long road and tough going. Even though my parents never had much money, they always made family time a priority. We did something as a family every Sunday. We went out to dinner pretty regularly as a family. We took regular vacations and weekend trips. Although this led to a lot of great family memories, it also led to a lot of tension when it was time to pay the bills and there was never enough money. It also led to my being teased mercilessly to the point of being ostracized in school for wearing clothes my mom bought at the bargain stores or for always being the last—if ever—kid to get the "new big thing" (and then having it be a knock-off brand that was supposedly "just as good" but really wasn't). All of this led to my, as an adult, always being very stressed making enough money to support the family but simultaneously being constantly tempted to spend more to buy the name brand or make myself feel good by spending. On the one hand, I carried on my parents great habit of putting family first when it came to money. On the other hand, my spending and near bargain-phobic inclinations often ended up at cross-purposes with my goals and sometimes added to my self-induced stress about being a provider.

Lisa says: My family was a different story. My dad worked for CBS and was one of the original producers of *60 Minutes*. He won two Emmys and a Peabody and regularly associated with Nobel Prize winners, politicians, and celebrities. Unfortunately, he passed away from an inoperable brain tumor when I was only five. Despite my dad's success, my parents didn't have a lot of savings, and my dad didn't have life insurance. I basically lost both parents at that time because my mom, who had been a somewhat reluctant stay-at-home mom until then, threw herself into work. At first, Mom's tendency to be a workaholic was driven by pure terror that we would lose our home, but even after she found success, she kept up the long hours because she found so much satisfaction in the workplace. Mom worked incredibly long hours and was very good at what she did, so we always had enough money. Even so, she was terrified to spend anything. Dad's unexpected death left us all with the feeling that something terrible was always just around the corner, and we'd better be ready when—not if—doom struck.

That meant saving as much and spending as little as possible. Where Greg's family was too generous for their resources at Christmas and birthdays, my family was reluctant to spend more than was absolutely necessary to get each other a token gift. As an adult, this left me with a real desire to take advantage of those experiences and acquire those things that would create family warmth and togetherness. But it also left me with a nagging anxiety and minor sense of guilt anytime I spent money—especially on anything fun. Looking at the bills was a traumatic experience every month even if there was enough money to pay them.

Greg says: Our first huge argument within the first few months of married life was about the phone bill. We moved away from Lisa's family so I could go to grad school. I had promised that I would do whatever I could to make sure she could visit or stay in touch with her family as often as she needed to. Ironically, after the first phone bill came, it was Lisa who got angry with herself for how much money she'd spent calling home. We still can't figure out how the fight got so big when I never complained about the calls and she was the one who made them! In retrospect, she was afraid that she couldn't trust either of us to check our spending. But there certainly wasn't any reason to fight about it. It just shows how easy it is to go a little crazy where money is concerned.

Lisa says: Together, we've worked hard to learn each other's stories and be sensitive to each other's financial woundedness. It would be the most natural thing in the world for Greg to become critical and judgmental whenever I got nervous about the bills or angry when I questioned, reasonably, I think, if it was really wise to make a particular purchase or plan a particular trip at this time.

Greg says: And I think it would have made total sense for Lisa to become exasperated and hostile whenever I wanted to take that weekend trip or purchase the more expensive item. We've had to learn to be gentle with each other, respect our strengths, tolerate each other's sensitivities, and keep checking our respective weaknesses against God's plan for our lives. Today, we've hit a pretty good balance. We still have our natural inclinations as far as money goes, but our reactions are much more in check, we've learned to really trust each other around money issues, and God has smoothed most of the rough edges off the tendencies that might otherwise have been our undoing. Together, with God's grace, we've found a way to create wonderful family memories and enjoy some security and savings. We've learned from each other and are happy to keep learning every day.

Money is never just about money. Taking the time to know each other's stories about money management and checking your feelings against God's plan for the treasure he has trusted to your care, no matter how small, can help you swim the fiscal tides without getting pulled down by the current. Speaking of checking God's plan for your finances, let's look at the next tip for curing money madness.

2. Pray about Your Finances

Since everything we have comes from God, it only makes sense that we should go to him to ask how he wants us to manage our money. Don't worry, we promise he won't ask you to give it all away! Remember what we discussed in the first part of this chapter? The Church teaches us that God wants us to have what us need to live a safe, secure life and to experience life as a gift. Of course, he wants us to remember to be generous to others, but that's different than saying that God doesn't want us to make good use of the treasure he gives us in our own homes.

When we bring our money-management decisions to God in prayer, it does three things. First, it helps eliminate the "whose way is the right way" competition many husbands and wives have about spending and saving. When you go to God with an open heart, it becomes pretty clear that you are more interested in learning his way than in getting yours, and that can really help lighten the tension between a husband and wife.

Second, praying about money management allows God to heal those parts of your heart that are financially

When you go to God with an open heart, it becomes pretty clear that you are more interested in learning his way than in getting yours, and that can really help lighten the tension between a husband and wife.

wounded. That little part of you that was teased by your classmates because you never wore the cool clothes? God wants to heal that. The fear that you will never have enough because, growing up, you didn't? God wants to heal that. The part of you that hates to even think about money because all your parents ever did was argue about it? God wants to heal that. Let him. Come to him in prayer, and let him teach you that dealing with finances doesn't have to include emotional drama of any kind.

Third, praying together about your finances helps remind you to continue to be sensitive to each other's perspectives and feelings about money even as you strive to bring your hearts more in line with God's when it comes to finances. It's harder to fight about the bills if you have taken the time to pray together first.

PRAYING ABOUT YOUR FINANCES EXERCISE

If you can't even begin to imagine what praying about your financial life would look like, try something like this.

> Lord, you provide for us every day, and we thank you for your generosity. Our hearts want and need so many things. Help us meet all the needs that bring us closer to you. Help us no longer want the things that would separate us from you or each other. Give us your wisdom to spend and save as you would have us do, and help us to remember to share some of what you have given us with those who are in need. We ask this in Jesus' name.

Of course, you should feel free to use your own words. The above is just one suggestion to get you started. If you're curious, the above prayer would fit nicely under the "S" in our PRAISE prayer acronym mentioned in chapter 3 (S—Seek his will). This might be one of many petitions you have in that category, but it's a good intention to remember. Learning how to be good stewards of the gifts God has given us is a lifelong process.

In addition to offering up your financial decisions in your daily prayer time together, be sure to pray together before making big decisions about your money and especially before any stressful money moment. For example, if paying the bills tends to cause you to argue, pray about it together before you pay the bills and ask for God's peace to rule the day. If you feel a little sick inside every time you check your balance online or at the ATM, pray about it before you log in or enter your PIN and after you get your receipt. Ask God to remind you of all the ways he takes care of you every day. If you can't make up your mind about which suit, or car,

> The most important thing is taking care of each other so that you both remember to solve the problem together instead of treating each other as the problem.

or house to buy, pray about it. It might seem silly, but God cares about everything you do. He gives us a lot of freedom to make our own decisions in both big and small things, but that doesn't mean he might not like to have some influence on the decision. Remember, God has numbered every hair on your head (Lk 12:7). Such a God obviously takes great interest in the little things in your life. Give him a chance to weigh in.

3. Use Your Problem-Solving Tools

Back in chapter 4 we reminded you that the most important thing in problem solving is, ironically, not solving the problem. The most important thing is taking care of each other so that you both remember to solve the problem together instead of treating each other as the problem. That's a great thing to remember when it comes to handling money.

There are two additional tips we would like to suggest to make managing your money more efficient. First, remember to use numbers, not feelings, to make decisions. Second, don't negotiate the "what." Always negotiate the "how" and the "when." Use numbers, not feelings.

⊕

Tom and Bethany argue almost every time Bethany makes a purchase. He says that she spends too much. She counters that she is always careful, but sometimes she can't resist buying something either she or the home needs, especially if there's a good sale. How do they work out their differences?

⊕

The bottom line is that Tom and Bethany need to use numbers, not feelings. It doesn't matter if Tom feels that Bethany is spending too much and Bethany feels that she isn't. It all comes down to the numbers. Do you have a good idea of what you have coming in and going out? Have you identified specific savings goals to the point that you know how much money you need to be putting aside to achieve those goals? Do you have a specific amount you have discerned needs to be set aside for charity? (This is where a financial planner can come in as really useful. If you don't have a financial professional in your life, bite the bullet and get one—more on that in a moment.) Assuming that you do, these numbers should be the arbiters of your discretionary spending, not your feelings. Once you have fulfilled your monthly financial obligations and your savings and charitable goals, you should feel free to use what is left over to make your lives a little easier or more enjoyable. Of course, you should discuss these purchases (or at least purchases over a dollar amount that you and your spouse predetermine), but overall you need to trust that each other is not trying to spend you out of house and home. We realize this isn't always a simple place to get to, but if you are doing the examination of conscience we described in point 1 and praying about money management as we suggested in point 2, you will not find this process to be as difficult as it may seem at first. The numbers tell you what you have. Trust the numbers, not your feelings.

Negotiate the "how" and "when," *not* the "what." This is actually a great rule for negotiating almost all differences of opinion. Everything we say about this in relationship to money applies to every other area of your life as well. The idea is that adults should be partners to each other, not parents. Parents need to tell children what is good and what they should or should not want because children are too immature to figure those things out for themselves. Hopefully, by adulthood, we all have a good enough head on our shoulders to know, basically, what we want and need. We don't need our partner behaving as a parent saying, "You want *what*? That's crazy! Why would you ever want to spend money on *that*?"

Speaking to your partner that way is what we call "Negotiating the 'what.'" In other words, any time you tell your partner what they should or shouldn't want, you have stopped being a partner and have begun acting as a parent. This is one of the quickest ways to get your spouse to hate you. No kidding.

That said, even though we all more or less know what we think is a good thing when we see it, we don't always know the best way and time to get it. That's what we need a partner for. We go to each other, not to ask permission for "what" we want, but to make a plan with our spouse to identify "how" we might go about getting it and "when" would be the most reasonable time frame. Say you want to remodel your bathroom. That's what you want. Your spouse needs to support you in that what. But say that your spouse also wants to put a fence up in the front yard, and you both want a vacation in the summer, but you don't have money for all of it. Now what? Well, first, you reassure each other that what you each want is important, and you are committed helping each other get it. Next, you start planning the "how" and the "when." For instance, since the bathroom is leaking into the basement, you need to do that sooner than later. But you might also decide to put aside some money now for that vacation plus decide you need to save another hundred dollars per month for the next few months to be able to make it a go. Likewise, although you can't afford the fence just yet if you do all that, you are still going to put thirty dollars per month in an envelope in your sock drawer so that you can begin saving for it. Even though it might seem as if it will take forever to save enough for the fence that way, it feels good to make the physical commitment to moving toward that goal. Plus, if you do manage to enjoy an unexpected windfall sometime in the near future, you will already have a good chunk of the money saved, and you can go ahead with your project at the first opportunity. Either way, you know that sooner or later you will both get all the things that are important to you through planning, cooperation, and commitment to each other's needs and heart's desires.

Compare this to arguing about whose wish list is more important followed by one of you just deciding that all the drama isn't worth it, so you give up on what you want, only to secretly resent your spouse for, once again, railroading you into giving up "everything" that's important to you. You'll see the benefits of the "Never negotiate the *'what'* but always negotiate the *'how'* and *'when'*" approach.

If you can remember to let the numbers guide your decisions and negotiate the "how" and "when" but not the "what" then—combined with prayer and the other tools we gave you in chapter 4—you will be well on your way to resolving whatever tension around money you and your spouse may be inclined to have.

4. Get Professional Help

You know that saying about how a lawyer who represents himself has a fool for a client? That goes double for money management. It doesn't matter how much (or how little) you think you know about money, or how much (or how little) money you have. Even a few sessions with a certified financial planner or at least a good accountant can help you establish a responsible budget, set realistic savings goals, establish what actually accounts for your discretionary income, and provide a reality check against your feelings when it comes to money. *We cannot recommend this highly enough.* As a general rule, the only thing parents talk to their kids about less than sex is money management. Most adults don't know the first thing about taking care of their finances. Even if you do have some financial skills, you need to face the fact that you are probably too close to your own financial situation to be sure your math really adds up. That's why physicians don't prescribe for themselves. They could. They just know it could lead to problems if they did.

Getting good financial advice early in your relationship can help you establish habits that will, literally, serve you well for the rest of your life. In addition to working with a certified financial planner, you might also get a great deal out of a program such as Phil Lenahan's Veritas Financial Ministries (www.veritas-financialministries.com), which is dedicated to helping couples apply a Catholic mindset to professional money management. In addition to budgeting, savings, and investment-planning resources, Veritas offers personal financial consulting by telephone and other personal finance training as well. Dave Ramsey's Financial Peace University is also quite good, although it comes from a more general Christian perspective as opposed to a more specifically Catholic one. The point is, there are great, faith-based resources available, and it is important to take advantage of them so that we can learn how to do the terrifically important work of managing our money the way God would have us do instead of what our feelings tell us to do.

There. That Didn't Hurt Too Much, Did It?

Most couples hate talking about money, but it doesn't have to be a negative experience. With a little practice and prayer, your financial conversations could actually be great avenues of grace, healing, and even togetherness. Take a little time to get to know each other's stories. Step outside your comfort zones, and be sensitive to each other's needs. Remember to use the good problem-solving skills you've been given as well as the ones you may naturally possess. Don't be afraid to seek ongoing training and professional help. Finally, give God the headship over your financial affairs, and he'll help you discover, step-by-step, what his plan is for managing the material blessings he has shared with you from his treasury.

CHAPTER NINE

Of Outlaws
and In-Laws

○○

"Catherine talks to her mom every single night—
for hours at a time," says Andy. "I don't have an
issue with her family. I *like* her mom. But I hate
having to compete with my mother-in-law for
my wife's attention. But anytime I try to bring
it up, she gets defensive and tells me that since
I'm not close to my parents I couldn't possibly
understand. The whole thing is so frustrating."

○○

"I can't stand Peter's mom," Allison says. "It
didn't start out that way. I really wanted his parents to like me. But she's just so mean! We can't

be together for five minutes without her criticizing something about the way I look, the way I
cook, or something I say. It all started when we
were planning our wedding. I don't think she
liked anything I did; my dress was "too fussy,"
the venue was "too far," the food was "just okay."
Why couldn't she just be a little nice? God help
me, I can't stand being around her. The worst
thing about it is that Peter just sits there and lets
it happen right in front of him! We fight about
it all the time. I don't understand why he won't
defend me."

◯◯

Tina complains, "I like John's family. They're
nice people. But I feel suffocated by his family.
My parents are divorced, so when we first started
dating, I loved the idea of big family celebrations
and togetherness. In fact, back when we started
going out, sometimes we'd even go to family
events on dates, and I really enjoyed it. But now,
every weekend is some cousin's birthday, some
family "tradition." If they do it once, suddenly
it's a "tradition," and we have to do it for all time
and all ages. It feels as if it can never just be us.
His mom is constantly inviting us to dinner. God
forbid I ever try to beg off just . . . because. She
acts as if I'm asking for her kidney. She gets sad
and pouty. 'But it won't be the same without you!'
I know. I sound like a horrible person, right? I
should be happy. They're really good people, and
they've totally welcomed me into the family. Most

of my girlfriends would kill for in-laws like mine. They actually *like* me—and don't get me wrong, I like them, too. I'd just like them even more if I saw them a little less. Keeping up with it is all just too much work."

⚭

The above situations are all examples of how in-laws can quickly become outlaws if you don't know how to manage the dynamics that occur when you marry into your spouse's family. Unfortunately, the Bible isn't much help here. On the one hand, we're told to "honor your father and your mother" (Ex 20:12); on the other hand, we're told that we are to leave our father and mother and join together as husband and wife in one body (Gn 2:24). How do you "cleave and leave" your family of origin but still honor each other's parents?

Marriage First

In chapter 7, we talked about the importance of prioritizing your marriage and establishing rituals and routines that will help make your relationship strong and see that it maintains good boundaries with the world. This would be a good time to go back and review the exercises we discussed in that chapter.

The best way to set boundaries with your in-laws is to not make the issue your in-laws. For example, Tina's problem above is not really that she has to spend time with her in-laws. The real problem is that she and John don't have enough of their own rituals and routines. They haven't figured out how much time they need as a couple every week and plotted that out on their calendar. Arguing about the in-laws in her case misses the point. She and John really have to sit down and figure out how much time they need for each other and what rituals and routines they need to establish to help protect that time. If your mother-in-law calls and asks you do to something Friday night, it's hard to say no if you don't already have a regular commitment to something else. Nature (and your mother-in-law) abhors a vacuum. If you don't want someone to take more time away from your marriage, make sure that you do something active and intentional to commit that specific chunk of time to your marriage; otherwise, someone or something is going to take it from you whether or not you want them to.

The same goes for Andy in the example above. He's frustrated that Catherine spends so much time on the phone with her mother. The problem isn't really Catherine's relationship with her mother, though. The real issue is that she and Andy haven't established rituals and routines to organize their evening. If they don't have plans, why shouldn't Catherine do what she wants with the unscheduled time? But if they had identified some evening rituals, things might be different. For example, if they had a standing agreement to have dinner every night around 6:30, and time to pray and talk, or play a game, or do something else they enjoyed starting each evening by around 8:30, Catherine would know that she could talk to her mom from about 7:30 to 8:30 every night while Andy had some time to do other things. Then they could get their time together. Andy's attempt to convince Catherine not to call her mom is a nonstarter unless they can be specific about how much time their relationship needs and what they plan to do with that time.

But What about Angry In-Laws?

Allison's situation with Peter's mother is a little different. Her issue isn't time but a personality clash. Who's to say if Peter's mother really is as horrible as Allison says or if Allison is either misunderstanding Peter's mom or being too sensitive in some way? It doesn't matter. Either way, they don't get along. The following strategies can help.

Decide When to Speak Up and When to Offer It Up

The truth is not every offense has to be dealt with. Sometimes it's best to let certain things go. But how do you decide? Generally speaking, if an issue is merely an offense to your comfort level or preferences, it's a good idea to practice the old Catholic habit of "offering it up." In other words, take the opportunity to be a better person by remembering that this might be a good opportunity to do your little part to foster the peace between men and women that Jesus sacrificed everything to make possible. What kinds of things might fall into this category? Things such as your mother-in-law bringing that soup you hate to your Christmas dinner, or buying too many (or too few) gifts for your kids, or how your father-in-law goes on about politics, or sports, or whatever hobby he might have, and other similar annoying habits are examples. Can these things and others like them be grating? Sure. Is it going to kill you to smile and bite your tongue? Despite how it may feel right now, the answer is "no." Let it go.

Also, while we're at it, please resist the urge to engage in any political, religious, or opinion-based conversation that doesn't have any practical effect on your life or wouldn't change anything even if you did change someone's mind. For example, let's say your in-laws belong to a different political party than you do. Does their political affiliation have any realistic or measurable impact on your ability to have a good relationship with your spouse or kids? Does it directly interfere with how you and your spouse feel God is calling you to live your life? Does arguing with them have any reasonable chance of changing their vote? No? Then keep it to yourself. The most you should say is, "Hmm, I've never thought about it that way before," and then change the subject or excuse yourself to use the restroom.

That said, there are many other times when you do need to say . . . something. For instance, if your in-laws' behavior (and this goes for your parents, too, by the way) does directly interfere with prayerful choices you and your spouse have made about how to organize your lives, raise your kids, or live your lives, then you need to politely thank them for their input but—again, politely—let it be known that this is something that you and your spouse have decided or will need to decide on your own.

Likewise, if your parents or in-laws directly try to undermine your faith, your relationship, your parenting, or your health or dignity as a person (for example, by directly insulting you or telling you in front of your children that your rules are silly, or insisting on serving food that you're allergic to, or insistently pressuring you to change decisions you and your spouse have made in prayer, or trying to undermine your spouse or your marriage), firm limits must be set.

OUR STORY

Greg says: For instance, my parents thought car seats were unnecessary for short trips to the neighboring farm when they were watching our children. We responded by putting our car seat in their car and telling them that if they didn't use it, as much as we loved them, they wouldn't get to watch the kids anymore. That didn't go over too well, but both the law and our kids' safety was at stake. I understood where they were coming from. I even had fond memories of lying on the shelf directly under the backseat window when I was about four, and laughing with glee when my dad stopped short and I flew off the shelf and bounced on the bench seat and onto the floor. Great fun. But that was a different time, and my mom and dad needed to respect our rules and the law.

Lisa says: Another example is, when my mom would go on a rant about how much she hated the Catholic Church, Greg would find a polite reason to excuse himself to use the restroom or, in the worst cases, invent a reason to go to the store or take a short walk around the block. And, although this never happened to us, we've talked to lots of people whose in-laws say cruel things or make nasty personal comments, and in these instances it's almost always best to say, "I'm sure you didn't mean anything by it, but I need you to tone things down or we're going to have to head out early."

Everyone puts their foot in it now and then, and if your parents or in-laws are basically decent people who usually try to do what you need them to do to support your relationship, then following up these times with a polite chat about what happened and how to work better together in the future will be the thing to do.

That said, often it's not so easy. When your folks aren't so agreeable, doing is much more important than saying. No one likes having limits put on them, and parents and in-laws will either get it the first time you explain yourself respectfully or they probably will never even after the hundredth time. Arguing is especially useless because it amounts to asking their permission to impose a limit on them. Who in their right mind would willingly consent to that? Of course, you should gently try to explain your concerns first. But if that doesn't work, don't throw good words after bad. Instead, simply take some reasonable action that eliminates their ability to commit that same offense again. Don't argue with them. Just do it. Did they do a poor job babysitting and argue back when you made your concerns known? Hire a sitter instead of calling them next time. Did they treat you horribly on your last visit and refuse to acknowledge that they could have done anything differently? Stay at the hotel instead of their home next time (or book them a room instead of hosting their visit). Is it hard to say exactly when they'll lose their cool and say something hurtful, but it always happens at some point during every visit? Next time, cut the visit short when that topic (or those comments) comes up again. If they get the message and apologize, give them another chance. If not, leave the boundary in place. Let their behavior, not your wishes or Walton-family fantasies, dictate the amount of closeness you can enjoy with them. Do as much as you can to be generous in this regard, but don't ever put yourself in the position of begging them to respect your concerns or accept your limits. Honoring your parents does not include allowing them to behave in a manner that is unbecoming to them or dishonoring to you or your children.

> Honoring your parents does not include allowing them to behave in a manner that is unbecoming to them or dishonoring to you or your children.

Who Sets the Limits?

Recall from the example at the beginning of the chapter that the other part of Allison's frustration with her relationship with her in-laws was Peter's inaction when his mom did something that she perceived as offensive. Remember her comment, "The worst thing about it is that Peter just sits there and lets it happen right in front of him! We fight about it all the time. I don't understand why he won't defend me."

It might seem crazy, but often it is genuinely the case that your spouse will not see the offenses his parents commit against you, and it isn't because he or she loves them more than you. In most cases, it is genuinely that, having been raised by these people, your spouse knows what those comments really mean, or what the intention behind that behavior really is, and he or she has learned to just put up with it. That doesn't mean that they should, necessarily. It just means that, having witnessed scenes such as this thousands of times growing up, it just isn't as shocking to your spouse as it is to you.

When the time comes to say something to your in-laws or set a limit with them, the thing you must never do is turn it into a test of how much your mate really loves you. The only thing that matters is that the words get said and limits get set by someone. (This is one of those "don't negotiate the 'what' but feel free to negotiate the 'how' and 'when'" times.) If your spouse genuinely doesn't see the offense or, for whatever reason, can't bring himself or herself to follow through, just handle it. Is it fair? Who cares. Grown-ups don't argue about "fair." They do what has to be done. Set the limit. Change the relationship with the in-laws; then process the results with your spouse.

But what if your spouse objects or tries to stop you? There are two possibilities. First, it may be that your spouse has some real insights that you need to hear. Do your best to be generous and listen to them. These insights should not be presented as excuses for his or her parents' behavior but rather insights that either help you see the behavior in a completely different light or give you an even better way to handle the situation than your original idea.

On the other hand, if your spouse's comments consistently attempt to justify his or her parents' behavior to the point where you feel that you are being told that you are crazy for wanting to do anything, or if your spouse tries to prevent you from taking even the most charitable actions to address your concerns, you may have a marriage issue more than an in-law issue. These kinds of behaviors represent a violation of the "don't negotiate the 'what'" rule. It would be perfectly acceptable for your spouse to suggest alternative ways to address a problem, especially if he or she has insights into his or her parents' behavior that you don't. That is just negotiating the how and the when. It is another thing altogether to try to prevent you from saying or doing something addressing the what. That prevents you from addressing the problem in a meaningful way.

It can be helpful in these times to point out to your spouse that you are not asking for his or her permission to address the problem, only his or her help in figuring out the best way to move forward. Likewise, you should politely but firmly insist that he or she either propose some useful ways to address the concern or he or she will have to live with how you choose to address it. In

such circumstances, it can be tempting to be as spite-
ful as possible in your intervention, just to show your
spouse and your in-laws that you won't be disregarded
that easily. Resist that temptation. Regardless of how
frustrated you get with your spouse or his or her parents, you need to be charitable in what you say and do. If
you're having a hard time figuring out what that means,
take it to prayer or talk things over with a mature person
whose advice you'd trust (as opposed to people you
know will agree with you whether or not you're right).

When You Need More Help . . .

We discuss many more strategies for dealing with difficult in-law situations in our book *God Help Me, These
People Are Driving Me Nuts!: Making Peace with Difficult
People.*[23] Of course, if in-law problems are causing you
and your spouse to treat each other with contempt or
engage in stonewalling (as we discussed in chapter 4),
you should consider seeking professional assistance. As
we noted earlier, most couples let problems fester for
four to six years before seeking help. Getting competent assistance early can prevent much bigger problems
down the road. See the resources listed in chapter 4 or at
the end of the book for competent help in dealing with
in-laws and other marital problems.

Coping with in-laws is easier for some than others,
but it's never simple. A little charity, a willingness to
be generous about differences in comfort or preference,
combined with the courage to set limits when necessary
and seek help if needed will eliminate the worst-case
scenarios and maybe, just maybe, allow you to enjoy
your extended families for once—or once again.

CHAPTER TEN

Holy
Sex!

In the first years of marriage, it isn't surprising that couples tend to have a lot of questions about sex. Marriage is, after all, the sacrament of sexuality (more on this potentially surprising fact in a moment).

Sex can be a challenge for every married couple because regardless of a couple's sexual history (according to one survey, about 80 percent of Catholics have engaged in premarital sexual relationships and approximately 20 percent are virgins at marriage), marriage takes the relationship to a new level. The relationship stakes seem higher in marriage—because they are—and that increased pressure can lead to certain challenges, confusion, and misunderstandings. For example, no matter your level of previous sexual experience, you may struggle with feelings of wondering why sex is suddenly "okay" just because you said, "I do," when, before marriage, it was clearly "not okay."

A couple may even confront some surprising awkwardness about their bodies or their sexuality. Couples who are virgins on their wedding day may understandably struggle with this, but even couples who have been sexually active prior to marriage may have difficulties with this contrast. As Pepper Schwartz, professor of sociology at the University of Washington observed, for many couples, premarital sex is about "being bad." Couples whose mindsets have unconsciously been formed by this attitude of "sex as naughty" often have a hard time figuring out how that model of sexuality fits into a relationship (marriage) where everything is supposed to be so good and even holy.[24]

Regardless of the sexual attitudes or experiences a couple brings to marriage, almost every couple finds that though their love for each other is still strong, their desire for sex may decrease as the tiredness, stress, or frustration of their busy lives start to wear on them. Similarly, many couples can be surprised by the awkwardness they feel about sexual intimacy. Couples who are not virgins often think that those sorts of feelings are reserved for less experienced couples, but marriage changes our mindsets about sex regardless of what we thought of it before. Finally, just as newly married couples have to work out differences with regard to handling all the tasks of daily life and negotiating different styles and preferences, many couples wonder how to handle disagreements about sex—for instance, arguments about frequency, about preferences, about positions, or other aspects of their sexual lives together.

Learning how to negotiate your different histories, attitudes, and preferences is an important challenge of the early years of marriage because the way you approach sexual differences will either build mistrust and resentment or trust and intimacy. Either way, the decisions you make now regarding your physical relationship establish patterns for intimacy in your marriage as a whole. This chapter gives you some basic tools for addressing these questions and more. Let's start with what sex actually means to marriage.

Marriage: The Sacrament of Sexuality

It comes as a surprise to many couples to learn it, but marriage is ultimately the sacrament of sexuality. You might not think of it that way right now, but it's true. A sacrament takes something common (water, bread, a man, a woman) and transforms it into a sign that conveys grace to help the people who encounter that sign become what God created them to be in this life and to help them get to heaven in the next. Blessed John Paul II taught that, in effect, there are only two times we experience love, itself, becoming incarnate: in marital intimacy and in the Eucharist. The Eucharist affects our nuptial union with Christ, and marital intimacy is a sign of that nuptial union Christ has with the Church (Eph 5:32).

While marriage involves many good things: working together, being friends to each other, enjoying times with each other, etc., it is ultimately lovemaking that serves as the efficacious sign (i.e., a sign that actually causes what it represents) of the couple's becoming one flesh. This is true both in terms of the physical union the couple experiences when they make love and in terms of their willingness to allow that love to be made incarnate in the form of the children they have and raise together. Sex unites two people into one, and children are a witness to the beauty of the love you share and a sign of hope to the world.

On another level, the Church teaches that love-making between a husband and wife is a physical sign of the passionate way God loves you both. The Song of Songs is a book in the Bible, not just because it is a beautiful love poem between a bride and bridegroom, but because the Church Fathers taught that it was a metaphor for the passionate love God has for his people. Pope Benedict XVI himself wrote that sexual love, when properly shared between a husband and wife, can be a source of transformation, transcendence, and perfection in virtue that helps couples not only in their love for each other but in recognizing Christ's love for each of them.[25]

Finally, a healthy, loving, marital sexuality challenges any fear or shame we encounter in the presence of vulnerability. Vulnerability is a dirty word to most people because it means the ability to be hurt. That's certainly one way to look at it, but having a healthy sense of vulnerability ultimately means that you are willing to lay down your defenses, pretenses, and preference for your own comfort zone to learn to really love and really be loved by your mate. Considering that we will spend an eternity being vulnerable in the loving presence of God in heaven—a God who sees every metaphorical bump and crease and wrinkle of our body, mind, and soul and still wants to love us. What better way to prepare for this otherwise terrifying reality than by confronting whatever fear or shame we encounter when our spouse looks on us in our nakedness and makes love with us. Sex unites. It creates. It serves as a prophetic witness of God's love for us. It transforms us and prepares us to stand confidently in the presence of a love so pure and passionate that we might be tempted to run from it if we weren't programmed by God to know better.

Huh? Why the Big Deal about Sex?

All this highfalutin talk about sexuality can be confusing for people because the world thinks of sex merely in terms of recreation. But we Christians think of sex as a re-creation of our wedding day, a restatement of our vows to one another in a language that transcends words and anticipates the nuptial union (nonsexual but still free, total, faithful, and fruitful) we will share with God in heaven. When the Church talks about sex, she is actually referring to an entirely different thing than the world thinks about when it talks about sex. Like diamonds versus cubic zirconia or "fool's gold" (i.e., iron pyrite) versus the real thing, the Church's vision of sex and the world's view of sex superficially resemble each other but couldn't be more different. In fact, what the Church has to say about sex makes no sense if you apply it to what the world calls sex—it would even be easy to consider what the Church says about sex to be offensive or absurd if you applied it to the worldly vision of sex. To really understand the Catholic vision of love we find it helpful to distinguish between eroticism (the world's vision of sex) and what we call "holy sex" (the Church's understanding of sex).

Eroticism versus Holy Sex

Superficially, eroticism and holy sex appear similar, but even with the one thing they seem to have in common—that is, they both feel good—there are radical differences. Eroticism feels good but can often lead to insecurity, doubt, shame, alienation, and heartbreak after. By contrast, holy sex feels terrific and leads to greater security, confidence, healthy vulnerability, and stronger unity after.

There are many other important differences besides the above. Holy sex unites two people, where eroticism can make people feel even more alone than before. Holy sex becomes more passionate and vital with time all on its own, while eroticism becomes boring without constantly looking for new experiences and props to "keep things interesting." Holy sex is driven by intimacy and friendship, while eroticism is driven purely by arousal. Holy sex is open to having children, but eroticism is terrified of children (mostly because, emotionally speaking, the lovers are often too childish themselves to want the competition). Holy sex leads to mental and even physical health, while eroticism is the cause of so much disease and death. Holy sex says, "I want all of you!" Eroticism says, "I only want the parts of you that make me feel good."

When you look at them side by side, holy sex and eroticism are two entirely different phenomena. It's important to realize, by the way, that even many married couples have not yet discovered holy sex. There are plenty of married couples who don't know that there is more to sex than using each other to scratch a hormonally driven itch. These are the couples who make wry jokes about how marriage killed their sex lives or how they don't have sex anymore because "that's just what happens when you've been married awhile." That is not what happens to couples who know the secrets of holy sex. Maintaining a joyful and satisfying marital sex life is never easy, but we find couples who have a holy sex mindset are just more motivated to do the work that keeps their physical relationship fresh and rewarding. But don't take our word for it. If eroticism was so rewarding, why would between 20 and 30 percent of all marriages be "sexless"[26] or "sex-starved"?[27] When sex is just another form of recreation (which eroticism tells us it is), it becomes just one more thing to do if you have the energy at the end of the day. But if a couple has a holy-sex mindset, they understand that sex isn't just an activity; it is an opportunity to celebrate the life and love they are creating together.

We want to make it clear that we are not saying that anyone who has struggled to understand or apply the teachings of the Church about sexuality in their marriage is a "bad Catholic" (any more, that is, than we're all bad Catholics—none of us get it perfectly "right" after all) or even a bad spouse. The real point, we would argue, is that couples who don't understand or apply the Catholic vision of love and sex in their marriage are depriving themselves of an opportunity to take things to the next level and don't even know it. Today, we'd like to invite you to learn the truth about holy sex and how to begin to celebrate in your marriage so that you can create a love life that will become more passionate with time, a love life that will become stronger because of the children you have together (rather than in spite of them), a love life that will enable you to satisfy the ache that every person has in his or her heart for a pure, free, total, faithful, and fruitful love.

Holy Sex: A Brief How-To

Our books, *For Better . . . Forever!: A Catholic Guide to Life-long Marriage* and, especially, *Holy Sex! A Catholic Guide to Toe-Curling, Mind-Blowing, Infallible Loving*[28] cover the topics addressed in this chapter, but we'll review some of the basic points to help you cultivate the habits that lead to a healthy, vibrant, lifelong celebration of holy sex in your marriage.

I. Prayer

You might be starting to notice a theme. . . . Everything in a great Catholic marriage begins with prayer. Initially, you might be tempted to think that prayer and sex go together like . . . well, two things that don't go together at all. But nothing could be further from the truth. As we pointed out earlier, Pope Benedict XVI and Pope John Paul II before him both taught that sex was given to us by God to be a transcendent and transformative experience that not only leads the couple to greater union with each other but also to greater union with God. Only couples who practice what we call "holy sex" know how to do this, however.

> Everything in a great Catholic marriage begins with prayer.

To foster your experience of the spiritual side of your physical relationship, we'd like to ask you to do two things. First we would ask you to write a "Lover's Prayer." It's a simple prayer that you say, not only before lovemaking, but at any time you feel the need to love your spouse a little better, a little more.

OUR STORY

Greg says: Of course, every couple should feel free to use their own words, but my Lover's Prayer goes like this, "Lord, help me to kiss her with your lips, to touch her with your hands, and to love her with your passion so that she might know how precious she is to both of us."

Lisa says: I have my own version of the Lover's Prayer. "Lord, help me to open myself to my husband's love. To receive him as I receive you. To draw near to him as I draw near to you and to love him as joyfully, willingly, and passionately as I love you so that he might know how wonderful he is to both of us."

We find that our respective Lover's Prayers have helped us to be more generous and attentive lovers in and out of the bedroom. The couples we have been honored to work with have told us similar stories. And why not? God gave the gift of sex to Adam and Eve and told them to "be fruitful and multiply." If God invented sex, then he would be the best person to teach couples how to get the most out of it and to use it in a way that helps them experience not only the fullness of pleasure but the fullness of intimacy and joy with each other.

We realize that this all might be a bit of a mental shift for many readers; however, that's why we'd like you to do the second thing, which is get more information. A good place to start would be our book *Holy Sex!*,[29] but in addition to that, we would point you to organizations such as the Theology of the Body Institute (www.tobinstitute.org) or individuals such as Christopher West (www.christopherwest.com) and similar ministries dedicated to disseminating the profound teachings of Pope John Paul II on love, sex, and marriage (known, collectively, as the Theology of the Body). We promise that what you learn from these resources will change your life and marriage in remarkable ways for the better. The more information you have to live the holy-sex lifestyle, the more you will experience God teaching you lessons about love that open your heart in ways you could never even imagine right now. But don't take our word for it. Go see for yourself. We know you'll be glad you did.

2. Be Patient

As newlyweds, you are discovering each other on a whole new level. Marriage challenges you to be truly vulnerable to another person. In the words of marriage educator Bill May, marriage "is the promise to make another person irreplaceable." Deciding that someone is truly irreplaceable to you can be as scary as it is exciting. It isn't unusual for newly married couples to feel a little bashful as they get used to being in the deep end of the grown-up-relationship pool.

CO

Beatriz and DJ have been married a little under a year. In the first few months, Beatriz found herself dealing with some feelings of nervousness and tentativeness around lovemaking. "It was weird," she says. "I have a really positive view of sexuality. I like my body and take care of myself. My parents never made me feel ashamed of talking about my body or sex. And I'm completely attracted to DJ. I was really looking forward to saying 'I do,' dragging DJ to the bedroom, and never coming out from under the covers again if I could help it! But things didn't quite work out as I thought."

DJ adds, "It was really strange. I mean, as she said, it isn't as if Bea is reserved or shy about expressing herself. But all of a sudden, when we were being intimate, it was as if she got all bashful and nervous. It was as if she was holding back. It really hurt. I wasn't sure if I was disappointing her as a lover or what. I felt a little let down, and a lot worried that things might not get better. I kept hearing all my friends and my dad's friends in my head joking about how getting married meant that all the passion dries up. I didn't want that kind of marriage. I never expected to be in that kind of marriage with Beatriz, but it sure looked as if that's where we were heading."

Beatriz says, "I completely get where DJ is coming from now, but I was frustrated at first, too. I didn't understand what was happening myself, so I couldn't really explain it to him. It was just as if new parts of my heart were opening up—kind of against my will almost—and it was really frightening to be this close being . . . needed by somebody else, and needing him just as much. It's hard to explain. I love him so much. I have since the first day he asked me out. But marriage really changed something for me. I was intimidated by how much my heart wanted to let him in. I'm just too used to being my own person for that. He's right. It did make me hold back just when I should have been giving him my all."

DJ says, "I think it would have been a disaster except for our prayer life together. Somehow we found the courage to be honest with each other in front of God about what we were going through. We'd pray together, and I'd ask God to help me be the friend and lover Bea needed me to be."

"And I'd pray that God would help me be as open to DJ as I wanted to be. It really helped," adds Beatriz.

DJ says, "I think being able to be honest with God and each other about what we were going through helped us be more patient with each other. I knew that Beatriz was really struggling, but struggling along with her in prayer helped me take it all a whole lot less personally."

Beatriz says, "I really noticed that. It really helped me to see how patient he was being, and it helped me not be resentful when he would feel as if I was holding back. Things have really turned around in the last couple of months. It's a lot more as I always dreamed it would be. We're being spontaneous and playful. It's just really great!" She looks at DJ, and he smiles knowingly.

Marriage will take your relationship to new levels, and while that's a really good thing, it can take some getting used to.

OUR STORY

Greg says: I remember in junior high swimming class, our final exam consisted of jumping off the high diving board. I liked swimming, but I was never the strongest swimmer and, at the time, I hated heights. I remember feeling a little sick to my stomach just looking at the board, much less climbing the steps. We practiced all quarter. Coach Duke did whatever he could to make sure we were ready. At the end of the class, when it was my turn to go off the diving board, I just remember all these thoughts going through my head. I knew I could do it. At least I was pretty sure I could. But it was nerve-racking nevertheless. My head was spinning and my gut was in knots even though a part of me was genuinely excited to do it. I said a quick prayer, something like, 'Please, God, don't let me die,'" and finally convinced myself to take my three steps forward and spring off the board and plunge headfirst in the water. Seconds later I was swimming with all my might to the surface. It seemed so far, and the cold water knocked all the breath right out of me. I broke the surface of the water and took a huge gulp of air. And I couldn't stop smiling. I couldn't wait to take another turn!

Intimacy—emotional and physical intimacy—in marriage is a lot like Greg's experience at the high diving board in junior high. Sure, it's awesome in theory, and sure, you've spent a lot of time preparing for it, but that doesn't make taking the leap any less terrifying. The trick is to be patient with yourself and each other. Trust the relationship you've built together. Remember the God who gave you to each other and wants to teach you what to do with the gift of your marriage. Don't take any feelings of fear or timidity personally. Just support each other through it and take the leap together. Being patient with each other while you get your heads around being husband and wife will allow you to experience the exhilaration that makes you want to keep going higher and deeper.

3. Be Intentional about Your Friendship

Where eroticism is driven solely by arousal, holy sex is driven by both arousal and, more importantly, friendship and intimacy. Arousal, being purely physiological, is susceptible to things such as exhaustion, stress, accommodation (getting used to each other), sickness, and other factors. That's a big part of the reason eroticism-driven sex dies in marriage.

But if you are truly working for each other's good as we described in chapter 6 on Lovelists and you take that effort seriously, then even on the days you don't feel as if you have anything left, you still want to find the person you know has your back and be as close to him or her as possible. You might not feel particularly "turned on" on a given day, but you will always feel the need to be close to your best friend. And, surprise, surprise, the closer you get, the closer you want to be.

⬭

Marybeth and Todd have been married for three years. They had their first child a year ago. It's been a year of blessings, and they love being parents to their baby boy, Jared, but over the past year their physical relationship has been pushed to the back burner with all the exhaustion and stress of healing from childbirth and late-night feedings and all the adjustments that come with adding another person to the household.

Todd says, "As much as it's hard to admit, when Jared was first born and Marybeth wasn't as physically available to me, it was tough for me. I mean, I felt guilty about the fact that it was hard for me; after all, it was my baby that was wearing her out, right? But that didn't make it any less difficult. I felt a little alone, and I really wasn't crazy about that feeling at all."

"I would see Todd getting a little quiet and withdrawn on those times I was too tired or touched out to make love. I love Todd, but I just wasn't used to carrying a baby all day and nursing and just always being 'on' like that," says Marybeth. "Don't get me wrong, I *love* being a mom, and I love Todd, too. But it was hard. The whole thing made me feel kind of resentful. As he says, it wasn't as if I was out partying without him or something. Being a new mom is tough work!"

Todd adds, "I knew that, but it took me a little while to get it into my head that being pouty or sullen wasn't exactly bringing my A game to the relationship and especially to fatherhood. I knew Marybeth needed to know she could count on me, and I just wasn't bringing it. I tried to shake off the whole baby-man routine. I really pushed myself hard to be a real friend to her, especially in those times when she was most tired. I'd try to do little things to show I loved her: make sure I took time with the baby, keep her company when she was up at night with him, and tell her how beautiful I thought she was. I especially worked hard at not coming off as if I was doing all that to get sex. I didn't want her to feel pressured by my loving her. It really wasn't about that—at least I really didn't want it to be. I just wanted her to know she could lean on me. I wanted her to know that I trusted her enough to know that we'd find our way back to being lovers as well as mom and dad."

Marybeth says, "That really meant a lot to me. When I saw Todd get over the pouting and really start being a friend with no strings attached, I think that took my respect for him and our friendship to a whole new level. He wasn't acting like another kid. He was being my man. It was really sexy—in a different, deeper way than I'd ever felt about him before. I've always been turned on by him, but this was just . . . more. Anyway, it made me try harder, too, even on the days when I was worn out. It made me want to be closer to him. I'd ask him if we could cuddle. I wouldn't neces- sarily be into having sex, but we'd be close, and I'd start thinking about how strong he was being

through the whole thing and one thing would
lead to another. . . . Things are really awesome
now. And I know it's because we've worked really
hard to be great friends through it all."

Marybeth and Todd's experience illustrates a common
recommendation of many sex therapists. Namely, when
your love life goes into a bit of a slump, getting closer
makes you want to be closer still.[30] But their experience
also highlights that it's hard to motivate yourself to get
past the tiredness, stress, and other obstacles unless
there is a part of you aching to be close to the one person in the world who is always looking for some way
to make your life a little easier and more pleasant. The
more you work on this friendship by working the Lovelist, using the respectful problem-solving strategies
we've outlined, praying together, prioritizing your
marriage, and so on, the more you will feel like true
friends to each other. And when it's time to go to bed,
even on those days in which the last thing you want is
to be swinging from the chandeliers, you will want to
be close to the person who has worked to stay close to
you all day. When your sexual relationship is driven by
friendship, your bodies speak a mutual language of love
and service that enable you to look at each other and
say, "See how we work for each other's good all day!
Even our bodies have learned to work for each other's
good!" and that's a very good thing.

4. Be Open to Life

Speaking of babies, it might surprise you to discover that having children together can actually take your love life to a whole new level—just as you saw with Marybeth and Todd's story above.

Of course, you might expect a Catholic marriage book to sneak that whole "open to life" thing in somewhere, right? Well, contrary to what you might think, the Church does not require you to plan on getting pregnant every time you have sex. It is true that the Church teaches us that we should not use any artificial means of contraception such as condoms or hormonal birth- control methods. It does so out of respect for your physical intimacy and out of a desire to see that you and your spouse have the healthiest, happiest, and holiest sexual life possible. Artificial birth control sends a message that is contrary to the generosity that lies at the heart of marital love. Contraception says, "I only want the parts of you that make me feel good, not the parts that really require a serious, lifelong commitment."

Being open to life is a blessing to marriage—and marital intimacy—because it communicates that no-holds-barred intention to make each other truly irreplaceable.

⚭UR STORY

Lisa says: One day I was reflecting on how much I love Greg. It was just one of those days when I just felt so full of love for him that I wished that every cell of my body could be completely wrapped up with every cell of his. And then it dawned on me. That's what our children are! Children are love's way of wrapping every cell of the husband's body around every cell of the wife's so that they can be completely and totally one with each other!

Greg says: That longing that each couple has to be totally one with each other is really never more perfectly fulfilled than when a husband and wife conceive a child in their love for one another. Having children isn't just about having children. It's the ultimate testament to the union between husband and wife.

There is nothing like having a child together in marriage that says, "We are truly 'all-in.'" Childbearing says, "We don't want our love to be a secret. We want the whole world to know that our passion for each other is so real . . . it's life-giving.

But if Catholics believe that having children is such a powerful sign of deepening intimacy and union, then why, you might wonder, does the Church encourage couples to learn and use Natural Family Planning to become more aware of their fertility? That's a big question, and we go into much more detail in *Holy Sex!* The short answer is that there is a huge difference between the ways artificial birth control and NFP work. Where birth control is really about closing your heart to God's plan for your family (whether consciously or not), NFP gives you the means of both postponing pregnancy and, when the time is right, conceiving a child.

When a couple uses NFP, they aren't just avoiding pregnancy. They are taking their sex life seriously—and we think most couples would want to take their sex lives seriously. NFP couples talk and pray about their physical relationship more than other couples, which leads to deeper intimacy in their lives overall. NFP couples ask each other and God every month if this is the month he is asking them to have a child or if, this month, he is asking them to work on strengthening some aspect of their marriage and family life so that they, the children they have, and the children they might yet have can enjoy the most peaceful, loving, stable, and satisfying home life possible. We aren't saying that couples who don't use NFP can't have happy marriages, but we are saying that people tend not to do anything they don't have to do. NFP makes discussing and praying about marriage a near necessity, and that bears tremendously good fruit both in the sex lives and the marriages of the couples who use it.

Being open to life certainly involves a willingness to see your unborn children in your beloved's eyes, but it is even more than that. It is, ultimately, a willingness to fully embrace the totality and intensity of what it means to give yourself completely to another person and make each other absolutely irreplaceable. NFP teaches couples valuable lessons about love, prayer, intimacy, and the spiritual meaning of both the body and lovemaking. To learn more about Natural Family Planning, we recommend contacting organizations such as the Couple to Couple League (www.ccli.org) to learn more about how NFP can be a blessing in your marriage and help you experience all the benefits associated with holy sex.

5. Never Settle

The last point we'll make on this is to never settle. The Theology of the Body teaches us that the ache in your heart for a free, total, faithful, fruitful love in and out of the bedroom has been given to you by God as a promise that he wants to fulfill, not just in the next life, but in your marriage today. Too many couples think that their desire for more intimacy, more passion, more . . . more, is just a romantic ideal that they have to surrender, so they stop working at it, especially if they hit a wall. Too many couples think that being married means settling for less love, less passion, less joy, less intimacy. It doesn't, and don't listen to anyone who tells you otherwise.

What is true is that pursuing these things takes real and consistent work, and sometimes it can be a challenge to sustain the effort it takes to have the marriage God wants you to have. Especially when it comes to sex, almost every couple can find themselves stuck from time to time. Couples regularly get into arguments about positions, frequency, what is and isn't acceptable, what they will and will not do. If these arguments go on too long, they feel a strong temptation to just give up because they feel they have gotten all they can get on their own power out of their marriage or sex lives together. The good news for any Catholic couple is that you don't have to rely on your own power. God's grace is available, and he wants to help you be the best lovers to each other that you can be. Why? He wants your love for each other to be a physical sign of the passion with which he loves you and because he wants the love you share to be a sign to the world that it is possible to have the great love everyone wants if people who desire that love will only draw closer to him to learn how to do it.

If you find that you and your beloved have hit an impasse and are feeling frustrated in your physical relationship especially, then please get faithful help. Begin by reading *Holy Sex!* together. Look into the Theology of the Body. If necessary, seek a faithful counselor (for those resources, please see the last chapter). You can have a joyful physical relationship that becomes more passionate your whole life long. God wants you to experience that kind of love together, and the Church has the resources and teaching to help you achieve it.

The good news is that by understanding the difference between eroticism and holy sex and beginning to cultivate the habits that make you a more prayerful, intimate, and generous couple, you will allow God into a part of your life that few couples have the courage to let him enter. The benefit to you is that he will, in turn, teach you everything he intended sex to be when he created it for Adam and Eve and all of mankind and womankind. He will show you how to love each other more perfectly, and, in the process, he will allow you to see a little more passionately how much he loves you, because he has given you as a sign of that love to each other.

CHAPTER ELEVEN

Bringing Up Baby?

One of the biggest challenges facing newly married couples is the question of when to have your first, or next, baby. Having children represents a major milestone for most couples, and there can be a great deal of confusion—if not outright tension—surrounding the question. Things can be especially difficult when a husband and wife disagree on the "best" time to have a child.

Hopefully, the question of having children at all does not represent a major point of contention, especially if you have been married in the Church. As a Catholic couple, you promised to receive children as a gift from the Lord as part of your wedding ceremony. This promise is essential to entering into a valid marriage as the Church defines it because children represent a visible sign to the world of the love you share—a love God wants the whole world to be able to experience— and allow you to bear witness to the world that life truly is a gift to be celebrated. "Children too are a gift from the Lord, the fruit of the womb, a reward" (Ps 127:3). But a willingness to receive children as a gift from the Lord doesn't necessarily clarify the question of when to start trying to have a child and how many children to have. How do you know? How do you decide?

∞

Bobby and Tara have been married two years. Tara would love to have a child, but Bobby isn't so sure: "I've just started a new job. I love the work, and there's real income potential in the future, but right now, I'm just not sure we can handle the expense, especially if Tara quits working even for a little while." Plus, Tara's dad's been in and out of the hospital a lot lately, and her mom has been a wreck. "We've been spending all our spare time either with her dad or her mom. With my schedule, Tara's work, and her dad's health, we're barely getting enough time together as it is. I'm not sure that we really have time to start a family right now."

Tara knows there are concerns, but she feels strongly about having a child anyway. "I just don't feel as if we should wait any more. I love kids. I don't want to have to wait any longer. Of course we need to be responsible, but I think if we just cut back a little we would certainly be able to make it. I could probably work from home at least for a while. I'm not sure why Bobby's so nervous. As for my dad, God willing, this is just temporary. I can't imagine his health problems being a long-term problem. I certainly don't think that's really a factor in whether we should start our family or not. Even with things being how they are, my parents would be thrilled to be grandparents."

Bobby and Tara have always had a good marriage, but this disagreement is causing them to fray at the edges. Tara asks, "How do you decide who's right? There really isn't any 'compromise' we can make. We either have another child or we don't. How do we decide who wins?"

CO

These are big questions. The good news is that there are a few simple steps any couple can use to resolve this issue in a way that guarantees that everybody wins.

Step One: What Does God Want?

As we've shared throughout this book, the first step to addressing any marital question is to find out what God wants by getting into the habit of praying together about God's will for your marriage and family—not just about your family size, but about every large and small decision of family life, especially family size. God has a plan for your family, and the closer your family reflects God's plan, the happier your family will be. Discerning that plan requires a husband and wife to pray together about all the decisions (big and small) in their lives.

Putting the Puzzle Together

It often happens that God gives both a husband and wife different pieces of the larger puzzle, expecting them through prayer and communication to cooperate with his grace to figure out how to put those pieces together and reveal his solution to their struggles. When couples do this, they not only solve whatever problem they're facing; they grow closer to each other and him (which is God's sneaky little plan all along). But to get to that place, the couple has to really work and pray together. For instance, it might be that, in his individual prayer times, Bobby feels that God is saying that addressing their financial and marital time crunch is serious enough to delay having a child right now. Meanwhile, in her individual prayer, Tara may feel just as strongly that God does want them to have a child sometime very soon. But these are not mutually exclusive realities. They may learn that they are both correct. For instance, it may be that God has a child in mind for them sooner than later, assuming that they can work together to overcome the obstacles that are currently in their path. Likewise, by working together to overcome those obstacles, they will not only arrive at a place where they can agree on the timing of their first child; they will have become better partners, better future parents, and better at discovering God's plan for their happiness in the process. In fact, one of the most important ways to make sure your marriage doesn't get lost in that crazy-busy, postbaby time is to enter into the discernment process of when to have your first child prayerfully, intentionally, and together. While it isn't unusual for one spouse to be more in favor of having a child sooner than the other spouse, it can become seriously problematic if one spouse constantly feels as if they are dragging their mate kicking and screaming down the road to parenthood. A commitment to praying together about this decision combined with a willingness to mutually engage all the reasonable concerns that might come up ensures that you are submitting your will to God's will and going through the discernment process as partners with God and your mate.

You'll never feel completely ready. Another point to consider is that no one ever really feels completely confident about starting a family. The simple fact is that you can't plan for every contingency, and you probably shouldn't bother trying. That's why we encouraged you to consider the most reasonable concerns instead of just saying to "lay out all your concerns." Bobby and Tara need to identify whether they really can live on the budget Tara is imagining. She needs to figure out if she really could work from home. They need to have at least a basic plan for how they'll get the time they need as a couple and, even more importantly, how they will respectfully communicate with each other if they ever feel as if like things are getting away from them. They may need to get a better sense of how serious her dad's health situation is and what Tara's mom may or may not need from them. These are examples of the reasonable concerns Bobby and Tara are facing. They're reasonable because they address observable, practical issues that are right in front of them. You'll never be able to completely overcome all the nervousness you may feel about beginning your family, so don't try. Just focus on

what is in front of you. Address those concerns. Pray.
Do what God is placing on your heart together.

Step Two: Practice Responsible Parenthood

Whether you are discerning the timing of your first or
next child, the Church offers some important guidance
in the form of its teaching on "responsible parenthood."
Responsible parenthood asks parents to remember that
being open to life isn't just about being open to concep-
tion. It also means being willing and able to do everything necessary to meet the needs of each age and stage
of the children you have and the child you want to have.
This way, every child in your care can grow up to be a
healthy person who knows how to love God, love others,
and demonstrate the virtues that help them experience
life as a gift—qualities such as joy, self-control, generosity, responsibility, and, of course, love. The Church
reminds us that every child has a fundamental right to
life and education.

Regarding this latter point, when the Church says
that parents are responsible for "educating" children,
she doesn't just mean teaching them reading, writing,
arithmetic, and a trade. The Church is primarily referring to parents' obligation to teach children how to love
God with all their heart, mind, soul, and strength and
love their neighbor as themselves. This fundamental
education in what it means to be a fully formed man
or woman of God is an incredibly important aspect of
responsible parenthood (see Sir 16:1–3).

The most important thing to remember in deciding
when to have your child is that it is your decision to
make, in prayer.[31] The Church says that only you—not

your mother-in-law, your friends, your parents, or even the Church—can for sure know whether or not you have the emotional, relational, and temporal resources you need to have a child and raise him or her to be a loving, godly person. Just keep in mind that this decision must also be rooted in a genuine desire to do what God wants you to do.[32]

The Blessing of Family

It is a truly wonderful thing to open your heart and home to all the children God wants you to have, especially when you can enjoy the fruit of your efforts in the form of a family that is remarkable in its ability to love God and each other. We have been blessed with such a family, and we can tell you what a powerful impact it has on the world. We have been so surprised how God has used our family to touch the lives of others. We've shared repeatedly how God wants to change the world through your marriage and family life, and we've been blessed to see what a ministry having a good marriage and family life can be. Just walking into a restaurant as a family who enjoys each other's company and is laughing together, with children who are respectful and polite to each other and know how to have fun in appropriate ways, is a powerful witness. We can't tell you how many unsolicited and completely unexpected comments we've gotten over the years from waitresses, hostesses, hotel managers, radio and television studio personnel (we often bring our children when we do interviews), and other strangers who say, "I've never seen a family who gets along with each other as you guys do! Your kids are so polite, so pleasant, and so

normal (i.e., they don't look as if the joy has been trained
out of them). What's your secret?"

Our secret is no secret at all. God has taught us how
to do it, step-by-step, by seeking his will in prayer and
learning how to cooperate with his grace by constantly
striving to learn new and better tools to create the marriage and family life he wants us to have.

We don't share this to say, "Look how awesome
we are." The point is that people aren't used to seeing
families that work, much less families that work well.
Your marriage and family
life, especially if you do
the work we describe in
our books, can be a pow-
erful force for good in the
world just by existing,
just by being an example,
not of a perfect family, but
of the kind of family God
wants everyone to have: a
joyful, loving community
of normal people who
genuinely show that they care for each other, enjoy each
other, and love each other. We can't tell you how much
seeing that means to people. Responsible parenthood
is the key to growing your family in a way that is a
blessing to you and to the world.

> **Responsible parenthood is the key to growing your family in a way that is a blessing to you and to the world.**

Step Three: Always Stay Open to What God Wants to Give

Even if you have decided that there are serious reasons to postpone having your first child, or your next

child, we'd like to join the Church in encouraging you to never put yourself in the position of saying, "That's it—we're done," with regard to having more children.

Your fertility is a gift from God, and as faithful couples we need to be willing to ask God to teach us how he wants us to use the gift of fertility. That will mean something different for every family. This is one area where practicing Natural Family Planning really helps. NFP encourages couples to pray and discuss their family life and family size on an ongoing basis so that you can discern what God's plan is for your family.

Even if you've decided that now isn't the best time to have a child or have your next child, consider praying about the following question on a regular basis throughout your lives together as a couple: "If we don't have those resources now, what do we need to do to get the additional emotional, relational, or temporal resources we believe are necessary to raise another child to love God and his or her neighbors?"

Why is this question so important? It's important for two reasons. First, this question gets couples out of those polarized "Should we or shouldn't we?" discussions. Using this question, the presumption is that you are committed to developing a plan to resolve the issues or acquire the resources (time, funds, etc.) that stand between you and the next child God may want to give you. The question isn't, "Do we have a child?" The question is, "What do we need to do to prepare for however many children God might want to give us?"

Second, by asking the above question, you'll be able to approach objections to the possibility of another child both realistically and generously. For instance, it may be that you decide that an older child's behavior or school problems—or the challenges you're facing in your life or marriage—require too much of your attention to be able to properly attend to a new baby at this time. But coming up with a plan to address those concerns becomes the way that you can both work to make your marriage and family stronger and more intimate while simultaneously remaining open to the possibility that, at some point when you resolve those issues, you may be ready to add another member to the family. Working together, you might discover that it really is possible to grow even closer together because of the children you have together rather than in spite of the children you have. Then again, it might turn out that the challenges you identify at some point in your life will take a long time to resolve, and it may never be time to have another child. But the point is that you are always working to make things better and always open to the possibility that things could change with God's grace and your hard work. Taking this approach, you will always remain open to life and do so responsibly, keeping in mind your mission, not only to be willing to have more children, but to raise your children in a faithful, loving environment that gives them the best education for living a holy life.

By following these three simple steps, it's possible to find the answers that were evading Bobby and Tara and other couples like them. Scripture tells us that all things are possible with God (Mt 19:26). It turns out that this applies to solving tough marriage questions as well.

CHAPTER TWELVE

Changing the World through Your Marriage

Throughout this book, we've mentioned that Catholics consider marriage and family life to be a ministry and that God wants to use your marriage to be a blessing to the world. We'd like to show you some additional ways your marriage could be a blessing, not just to you, your spouse, and your children, but to the whole Church.

When a couple chooses to be married in the Catholic Church, they are not only publicly acknowledging their earthly commitment to each other, but they are also stating to the world that they believe God has chosen them for each other—to be each other's best hope for both becoming what he created each of you to be in this life and helping get each other to heaven in the next. In a sense, you have been chosen to play an essential role in your partner's perfection, second only to the saving

power of Jesus Christ and your mate's free acceptance
of God's grace. Your job is to unfailingly support, lov-
ingly challenge, and consistently encourage each other
to be faithful to God's plan for helping you become
saints.

Chances are you might feel a little intimidated by
the idea of becoming saints. That's okay. It is a tall
order. But you don't have to worry. God promises to
give you everything you need to be the faithful, loving, godly people he cre-
ated you to be, and he
will use the simple tasks
of your everyday mar-
riage to accomplish that.
You don't have to travel
to far-off places or work
miracles to be a saint—
thank heavens! You just
have to be willing to fulfill
the promises of your mar-
riage vocation every day;
to exemplify a love that is
free, total, faithful, and fruitful; to work daily to create
deeper communion between yourselves; to accept children from the Lord and do your best to raise them to be
godly people; and to commit to generously working for
each other's good by willing to love each other more
than you love your own comfort zones. If you do your
best to work with God's grace to accomplish those simple but profound promises, you will be walking what
St. Thérèse the Little Flower called the "Little Way" to
holiness. You won't do it perfectly. And that's okay. You

> Your job is to
> unfailingly support,
> lovingly challenge,
> and consistently
> encourage each
> other to be faithful
> to God's plan
> for helping you
> become saints.

just have to be willing to try to walk the path the best you can with God's help.

Some of you might be saying that this seems like a whole lot of religious stuff you weren't planning on being a part of your marriage, but there is actually a significant body of research that shows that couples who have a both a shared set of values and a shared commitment to supporting each other as they strive to live up to those values have happier, more stable, and more rewarding marriages than those couples who have less of a commitment to shared values.[33] Additional studies have shown that the more clearly defined a couple's beliefs and values are and the more consistently that couple helps each other be more faithful to those values and beliefs, the happier that couple is.[34] It makes sense. If you notice that day by day you are actually doing a better and better job of living up to your beliefs and values in large part because of your spouse's encouragement, of course you'd be grateful for your spouse's support. Of course your marriage would benefit from that support and gratitude. Over the next few pages, we're going to show you how to cultivate that pursuit of what marriage researchers call "shared meaning and values" in a way that helps you be a more faithful and a more intimate and happy couple.

Shared Meaning and Your Vocation

The Church considers marriage a vocation, a call to follow Christ in selfless service and to work for the good of God's family, the Church. As you do the hard, but joyful, work of fulfilling the commitments we described above, you are not just working for each other's good;

you are working for the good of the whole Church as well. How? You do so in two ways. First, as we have already shared, marriage works for the good of the whole world by providing a witness of God's love, by giving the world an icon of what God's free, total, faithful, and fruitful love looks like this side of heaven, and by giving children a loving, stable, nurturing home in which they can be formed in all the virtues that enable them to live life as a gift.[35] When you commit to these things, you're not only working for the good of your spouse but you're also working for the good of the whole world. That is to say you are faithfully living out the vocation that is your marriage—that call to follow Christ and generously offer yourself in service for the good of all people. We hope that you know at least a few couples whose love makes the world a little better for the rest of us, too. The Church wants you to be another example of that kind of love.

What you've been learning about so far constitutes the basis of every couple's marital vocation. But in addition to these basic tasks of the marital vocation, there is a second way God wants to change the world through your marriage. Whether you are aware of it or not, God is also trying to send the world a particular message through you. That message is called a "charism." A charism is the particular message, or gift, that God wants to give to others through your particular relationship.

If you've heard the word "charism," you might have heard it in reference to various religious communities. For instance, every religious order (e.g., the Benedictines, the Jesuits, the Dominicans, the Franciscans, etc.) has a charism—a particular work or mission (such as preaching, teaching, hospitality, or caring for the sick)—that benefits the world in a particular way. Each of these orders lives out their general vocation to religious life in a generally similar way (for instance, they all pray and live lives of chastity, obedience, and service), but their charism—the specific work they do in the world or message God is trying to send to the world through them—differs greatly from order to order. It becomes the particular work or message most closely identified with why God called that particular group of men or women together as opposed to any other group of people wanting to live a life of faith.

Now, truth be told, you don't absolutely have to know your specific charism now or even ever. It is enough to commit to living out your basic vocation as a married couple. In fact, it is more than enough. But for couples who want to discover a little more about God's plan for their particular lives—why he brought the two of you together instead of you and anybody else—and experience greater intimacy and stability because of the shared meaning you have in your relationship, you might want to begin prayerfully considering the charism that God wants you to live out in your marriage.

Think of it this way. Imagine some couples you know. You could probably describe those couples in a few words or a sentence at most. Some of those descriptions are good and, probably, some are bad. "Juan and Jacinta? Oh, they're always doing some kind of community service." "Bob and Gina? I've never known a couple who loved their kids more." "Mark and Catherine? They bicker all the time." "Peter and Melinda? They're obsessed with their careers."

As we said, some of those descriptions are good, some bad. Regardless, these descriptors constitute the messages these couples are sending to the world whether they know it or not. Some of those messages are uplifting (service, family devotion) and some are not (bickering, careerism). Your marriage will inevitably send a message to the world, too. It is unavoidable. Part of the ministry of marriage is recognizing the fact that people will watch you and learn from you. Whether you want them to or not, whether you care if they do or not, people will either be challenged and inspired by your love or be saddened and diminished by your example. The good news is that you have the power to control the message you send to the world. In fact, God wants to help you do it because he wants your message to the world to be his message to the world. That's what it means to be a Christian witness as all Catholics are called to be. The uplifting, grace-filled message that God wants to send to the world through your life of love together is called a charism.

So, how do you go about discovering your charism? Well, first of all, relax about it. It will become more obvious to you the more you work through three things:

prayer, generous service to each other, and reflection and practice of virtue. Let's take a brief look at each of these.

Prayer

By now, you won't be surprised that prayer is the first step in discerning your marital charism. Understanding your charism represents a deepening of your understanding of God's plan for your marriage. In order to truly understand what that plan is on every level, it will be really important to learn how to pray, both individually and together as a couple, so that God can help you discover and live according to the message he wants to send to the world through your lives. Even if you have never prayed, or never prayed together before, we would respectfully ask you to revisit the chapter on prayer (chapter 3) and begin this very important practice so that you can discover all the wonderful things God has in store for you and your marriage.

Mutual Service

Throughout the book, we've discussed different ways you and your spouse can work for each other's good. The commitment to generously work for each other's good is another important way of discovering your charism, the message God wants to send to the world through your life of love together.

Both you and your partner will ask many things from each other. You will ask for help, for affection, for little acts of service that make each other's lives easier, more grace filled, more pleasant. Sometimes the things your partner asks of you will seem hard. Sometimes you will want to say no, or, "That's just not me. Don't ask me to do that." We are going to ask you to consider a different approach. Assuming that your partner isn't asking you to do anything that is objectively immoral, we would ask you to say yes to your partner's requests—even the ones that seem hard and challenge your comfort zone. Why? The needs and desires on your spouse's heart are actually an invitation to you from God to grow in ways you would never grow on your own. By responding generously to those requests, big and small, easy and hard, you will start to discover the many ways God is calling you to live out his plan for your life together, and you will slowly reveal the charism he has in mind for you.

⚭

Chuck and Marlena have been married five years. They aren't wealthy, but they have enough to meet their needs, and because of that, they do what they can to give back to the community. Chuck says, "Marlena has really opened my heart to seeing the needs of other people. I don't think of myself as having been selfish before, but I also can't say I was really clued in to what was going on around me."

Chuck and Marlena spend one Saturday a month with their kids volunteering at the local soup kitchen, and they find little ways to benefit a few other local community charities through their small donations or acts of service. Their friends know they can always be counted on when help is needed.

Marlena says, "I didn't have a lot growing up, and it's just important to me to help where we can. I know we can't fix everyone's problems, but we can do something to help. I really appreciate Chuck's willingness, not just to let me do some charitable things, but to join me in it."

"To be honest, it wasn't easy for me," Chuck adds. "I prefer to have my weekends to myself. Plus, I'm a big saver, so the more I can put away the happier I am. But Marlena has been really good about making a savings plan with me that I can live with. I have to say that, thanks to her, I really feel as if I'm becoming a more caring person, and I really like who I'm becoming. I like who we're becoming."

Chuck and Marlena's charism of "responsible service to their community" came from their willingness to learn from each other what it meant to live out their shared values. Marlena's generosity inspired Chuck to stretch himself in ways that were a little uncomfortable, but still good. Similarly, Chuck's fiscal responsibility encouraged Marlena to be generous in a way that was responsible and was respectful of their personal goals. Their willingness to learn from each other helped them find new ways to live up to their values and beliefs together.

⚭

Reflecting on and Practicing Virtue

Most people think of virtue as something that helps them be good people. That's true. But what most people don't know is that psychologists tell us that virtues such as love, generosity, peace, patience, courage, and so on, make us happy. Studies in the field of positive psychology teach us that the more a person tries to be virtuous, the happier they are with themselves, their life, and their relationships.[36] Of course, Christians have also taught this long before anyone thought of doing research in positive psychology.

A virtue is a quality that helps you take whatever life throws at you and use it to become a better, stronger, more loving, more humane person. Below are some examples of virtues. You can probably think of others.

VIRTUE EXERCISE

Go through this list and put a check mark beside the virtues you see in your spouse and a star beside the virtues you know you possess.

FAITH	HOPE	LOVE	BALANCE
PRUDENCE	JUSTICE	STICK-TO-ITIVENESS	GENEROSITY
PATIENCE	PEACE	KINDNESS	DEVOTION
KINDNESS	COURAGE	TRUSTWORTHINESS	WISDOM

It might seem strange or super-religious to think about discussing virtues as a couple, but that's because most people just aren't used to doing it. The fact is study after study in positive psychology has shown that the more people are aware of the role virtue plays in their life and support each other in living virtuously, the happier they are as individuals and couples.

The more you learn to talk to each other about the virtues that seem to come up most often as you pray together, learn from each other, and just live life together in general, the clearer your charism will become. Let us offer some examples.

CD

Luz and Max love to entertain. The virtue of hospitality is very important to them. They work hard to make their home a warm, welcoming place for themselves, their children, their friends, and their children's friends. They like that their home is known in the neighborhood as a safe, fun place for kids to hang out and parents to come for dinner and hang out. Hospitality is their charism, and they love supporting each other in this very important virtue.

CD

John and Elena love their faith. They both teach in their parish's religious education program, and they help out with some of the adult faith-formation classes, too. Faith is an important shared virtue and is the core of their charism of parish ministry. Whenever their pastor needs help with a parish program, they're the first couple he thinks to ask.

⚭

Dan and Tracy have a real heart for justice. They react strongly when they see a person who is suffering, and they try to do what they can to help out. They sponsor a few children through a charity that provides food, shelter, and education for children in third-world countries. When a local family is going through a tough time, Dan and Tracy are usually the ones calling up neighbors and friends to organize meals or arrange for grass-cutting or childcare for the family who is having difficulties. Their charism is care of their neighbor and charity.

⚭

These are just a few examples. The point is marriage is a vocation in which a couple is called to serve each other and their church and community. You are God's gift to each other, but you are also God's gift to the world. All Christians are called to serve. Your willingness to serve each other and to serve the Church or community in some way, however big or small, represents your commitment to live out your vocation. The special things you do to live out your vocation represent your charism. Eventually you will share your charism with your children, as they learn what it means to build God's kingdom by watching you live your charism and, even better, working at your side in whatever ways they can.

When you make a commitment to serve each other and your church or community, you help each other grow as persons. You help each other be a better couple. And you become an even better example of God's love for the world as he loves the world through you.

CHAPTER THIRTEEN

Staying in Love for Life: Additional Resources

Marriage involves a lot of "on-the-job training." No matter how good your marriage preparation was, nothing can really prepare you for the reality of marriage. As we bring this book to close, we wanted to leave you with some suggestions that will make your life together as smooth as possible for years to come.

Don't Panic

The most important thing you need to remember now is that while there will be many opportunities to celebrate and rejoice in your marriage, there will also be many times that you have no idea what you are doing, how you ended up in this mess, and how you are going to get through it without killing each other. Repeat after us. "This is perfectly normal."

When you find yourself in these spots, the first thing you have to remember is that the frustration, fear, and even hopelessness you may feel is perfectly normal. No matter how much you love each other, no matter how great you are together, no matter how fantastic your families of origin were, and no matter how many skills you think you have, there will come many points in your marriage when you hit a wall and cannot see how you are going to get over it. Every couple goes through it. Honest. We mean it. Take a breath. It will pass. Just keep working on it. You will be fine.

Pray, Pray, Pray

While we're on the subject, one of the ways to keep from hitting that wall in the first place and getting over those walls more quickly when you do run into them is prayer. Pray together every day, pray together before serious discussions, and pray together when things start heating up. It's hard to hold on to your anger when you sincerely put yourself in God's presence, and letting go of the anger allows you to open up to new possibilities that God might be leading you to.

Be Humble and Keep Learning

In any job, regular training is a necessary part of a successful career. The same is true of marriage. Make a promise to each other that you will faithfully and regularly take advantage of good, faithful resources to help you continue to discover what it means to experience the love God meant you to live.

The following are some great resources you should be aware of to help you learn more about God's plan for marriage and how to grow together in love, happiness, and holiness.

The Couple to Couple League—Ongoing education and support for the successful practice of the art of Natural Family Planning. Learn more at www.ccli.org.

For Your Marriage—A marriage ministry by the US Conference of Catholic Bishops. A great web portal with lots of articles, ideas, books, and resources to help you discover the love you were meant to live. Learn more at www.foryourmarriage.org.

Retrouvaille—Weekend retreats and follow-up sessions for couples who are having some difficulties. Retrouvaille is a peer-led couples ministry that teaches communication and conflict-resolution skills and helps couples rediscover their love and commitment. Learn more at http://www.retrouvaille.org.

The Theology of the Body Institute—Take your physical relationship to the next level by discovering God's plan for sexual love. Learn more at www.tobinstitute.org.

Worldwide Marriage Encounter—Weekend retreats for married couples. Learn new skills and discover new ways to let God into your marriage and grow closer to each other. Learn more at www.wwme.org.

Get Help Early

Research shows that on average couples don't contact a marriage counselor until they've been struggling for four to six years! That's a lot of time to waste in conflict.

Getting help early can prevent serious resentments from undermining your relationship.

The fantastic news is that more than 90 percent of couples who seek professional marital counseling heal their marriages. Just be certain to work with someone who is a trained, marriage-friendly therapist. Although many individual therapists say they do marital therapy (because they sometimes see couples), they are not necessarily trained in marital therapy. You should look for a therapist who is either a member of the American Association of Marriage and Family Therapy, or has been trained by the Gottman Institute, or is a professional member on www.marriage-friendlytherapists. com. These therapists have been trained in research-based methods of marriage counseling that offer you the best chance of success. To locate a professional marriage therapist, the following resources can be helpful.

American Association of Marriage and Family Therapists—A professional society for trained marriage and family therapists. Offers nationwide referrals to local AAMFT member therapists. Learn more at www.aamft. org.

Gottman Relationship Institute—One of the world's premier training institutes for empirically based marital therapy. Offers international referrals to local marriage therapists trained by the Gottman Institute. Learn more at www.gottman.com.

Marriage Friendly Therapists—A national referral source for marriage therapists trained and committed to helping couples find the skills to stay together. Learn more at www.marriage-friendlytherapists.com.

The Pastoral Solutions Institute—Directed by Greg and Lisa Popcak, this organization provides Catholic marriage counseling via telephone to couples around the world. See their website (www.catholiccounselors. com) for books and other resources, or call 740-266-6461 to make an appointment with a professional Catholic therapist.

Read Great Books on Marriage

Even if you never avail yourselves of professional help, you would be wise to commit regular time to reading good marriage self-help books. Not all of them are created equal, of course. Try to stick to the books that are rooted in research or present a solid Catholic perspective. Regardless of the book you choose, the two of you won't always agree with everything it says, but that doesn't matter. What matters is that you are learning and discussing your marriage, and that's always a good thing. If you enjoyed this book, you might check out our other marriage resources, *For Better . . . Forever!* and *Holy Sex!* We also highly recommend any marriage books by John Gottman, Bill Doherty, or Michelle Weiner-Davis. While these books do not look at marriage from a Catholic perspective per se, they are rooted in solid research in what makes good couples work well together and how to teach that to couples who want to make their marriages better.

God Grant You Many Blessed Years!

As this book draws to a close, we want to wish you all the best in your future years together. Whether you know it or not, God wants to do a great work in your hearts and home. Nothing will stop him from giving you the marriage of your dreams if you continually bring your relationship to him and constantly discover new and better ways to love each other and cooperate with his grace. No matter where you come from, no matter what you do or don't have, God wants to do great things for your marriage so that he can change the world through your marriage.

Over the course of your many years together, all the things you promised to love each other through on your wedding day—the good times and bad, sickness and health, wealth and hardship—will probably happen. Sometimes you'll even drive each other crazy. All of this is perfectly normal. Just remember Douglas Addams's famous advice in the *Hitchhiker's Guide to the Galaxy*, "Don't panic." Or if you prefer St. Paul, just remember that all things work to the good for those who love God (Rom 8:28), and you can accomplish all things when Christ is your strength (Phil 4:13).

This book began with good news, and it ends with good news. God wants you to have a great marriage, and if he is for you, who can be against you? Give your marriage to God every moment of every day, commit to loving each other no matter what, and you will create—with his help—a marriage that will make the angels smile and the neighbors sick with jealousy. You will be the couple that everyone wants to be, the couple whose kids and grandkids hope they can one day be like. Your love will be a light to the world—a testament that the ache at the center of everyone's heart for a free, total, faithful, and fruitful love can be fulfilled. The world will know that kind of love is possible, because they will see it in you.

Notes

1. K. Heller, "The Myth of the High Rate of Divorce," *Psych Central* (2012). Available online at http://psychcentral.com/lib/2012/the-myth-of-the-high-rate-of-divorce.

2. J. Gottman, *Why Marriages Succeed or Fail*, (New York: Simon and Schuster, 1995).

3. W. B. Wilcox and E. Williamson, "The Cultural Contradictions of Mainline Family Ideology and Practice," in *American Religions and the Family*, eds. Don S. Browning and David A. Clairmont (New York: Columbia University Press, 2007); C. A. Johnson, S. M. Stanley, N. D. Glenn, P.A. Amato, S. L. Nock, H. J. Markman, and M. R. Dion, *Marriage in Oklahoma: 2001 Baseline Statewide Survey on Marriage and Divorce* (Oklahoma City: Oklahoma Department of Human Services, 2002): 25-26.

4. S. Wolpert, "Here's What Marital Commitment Really Means," UCLA Newsroom (2012). Available online at http://newsroom.ucla.edu/portal/ucla/here-is-what-real-commitment-to-228064.aspx.

5. John Gottman, and Nan Silver, *Seven Principles for Making Marriage Work*, (Crown, 2000).

6. S. Sassler, "The Specter of Divorce: Views from Working and Middle-Class Cohabitors," in *Family Relations* 60, no. 5 (December 2012): 602-616.

7. Gregory K. Popcak, *For Better . . . Forever!: A Catholic Guide to Lifelong Marriage* (Huntington, IN: Our Sunday Visitor, 2009).

8. John Gottman and J. S. Gottman, "Bridging the Couple Chasm," Gottman Couple's Therapy: A New Research-Based Approach. A Workshop for Clinicians (The Gottman Institute, 2012).

9. Second Vatican Council, *Gaudium et Spes* (1965). Available online at http://www.vatican.va.

10. *Catechism of the Catholic Church*. (US Catholic Church, 1997), 2565.

11. F. D. Fincham, N. M. Lambert, and S. R. H. Beach, "Faith and Unfaithfulness: Can Praying for Your Partner Reduce Infidelity?" *Journal of Personality and Social Psychology* 99, no. 4 (2010): 649-659.

12. Andrew Greeley, *Faithful Attraction* (New York: TOR, 1991), 292.

13. S. Rushnell and L. DuArt, Couples *Who Pray*. (Nashville: Thomas Nelson, 2011).

14. R. A. Emmons, and M. E. McCullough, "Counting Blessings Versus Burdens: An Experimental Investigation of Gratitude and

Subjective Well-Being in Daily Life" in *Journal of Personality and Social Psychology 84*, no. 2 (2003): 377-389.

15. Gregory K. Popcak, *The Life God Wants You to Have* (New York: Crossroads Publishing Company, 2011).

16. If either a single spouse's temper or a couples' arguments regularly exceed an 8 or higher on this scale, it would be important for that spouse and/or the couple to seek professional assistance. Couples may contact the Pastoral Solutions Institute ro learn more about resources and approaches to healthy conflict resolution by calling 740-266-6461 or visiting us online at www.catholiccounselors.com.

17. Popcak, *For Better . . . Forever!*

18. B. Fiese, T. Tomcho, and M. Douglas, et al., "A Review of 50 Years of Research on Naturally Occurring Family Routines and Rituals: Cause for Celebration?" in *Journal of Family Psychology 16*, no. 4 (2002): 381-390.

19. Gottman and Gottman, "Bridging the Couple Chasm."

20. *Catechism of the Catholic Church*, 2434.

21. Ibid., 2403.

22. Pope Leo XIII, *Rerum Novarum* (1891), 36.

23. Gregory K. Popcak, *God Help Me, These People Are Driving Me Nuts!: Making Peace with Difficult People*. (Chicago: Loyola Press, 2001).

24. Pepper Schwartz, Peer Marriage: *How Love Between Equals Really Works* (New York: Free Press, 2003).

25. Pope Benedict XVI, *Deus Caritas Est* (2005).

26. M. Weiner-Davis, *The Sex-Starved Marriage*. (New York: Simon & Schuster, 2003).

27. Mauer, E. D., "The Big No: The Truth about Sexless Marriages," *MSNBC News*. sec. Today Show Relationships, September 8, 2009. Available online at today.msnbc.msn.com.

28. Gregory K. Popcak,. Holy Sex!: *A Catholic Guide to Toe-Curling, Mind-Blowing, Infallible Loving* (New York: Crossroad Publishing, 2008).

29. Ibid.

30. Weiner-Davis, *The Sex-Starved Marriage*.

31. *Guadium et Spes*, 50.

32. Ibid.

33. Gottman and Gottman, "Bridging the Couple Chasm."

34. W. B. Wilcox, "When Baby Makes Three. How Parenting Makes Marriage Meaningful and Marriage Makes Parenting Bearable" (The National Marriage Project, University of Virginia, 2011).

35. Pope John Paul II, *Evangelium Vitae* (1995).

36. M. Seligman, *Authentic Happiness* (New York: Free Press, 2003).

Index

Gregory K. Popcak is executive director of Pastoral Solutions Institute and the author of over a dozen popular books integrating Catholic theology and counseling psychology. He is an expert on the practical applications of the theology of the body. Popcak's books include *For Better . . . Forever!*, *Holy Sex!*, and *Parenting with Grace*. Popcak is a regular contributor to *Catholic Digest*, *Family Foundations*, and others. Since 2001, he and his wife and coauthor, Lisa Popcak, have hosted several nationally syndicated radio advice programs, including *Heart, Mind and Strength*, *Fully Alive!*, and, most recently, *More2Life*. They have also hosted two television series for EWTN: *For Better . . . FOREVER* and *God Help Me!* He serves as an adjunct professor for the sociology and graduate theology departments at the Franciscan University of Steubenville. He also serves as adjunct faculty for the Harold Abel School of Social and Behavioral Science at Capella University.

Lisa Popcak is the vice president of the Pastoral Solutions Institute. A family life coach, lactation consultant, and professional educator, she is the coauthor of *For Better . . . Forever!*, *Holy Sex!*, and *Parenting with Grace*. Since 2001, she and her husband and coauthor, Gregory Popcak, have hosted several nationally syndicated radio advice programs, including *Heart, Mind and Strength*, *Fully Alive!*, and, most recently, *More2Life*. They have also hosted two television series for EWTN: *For Better . . . FOREVER* and *God Help Me!* Popcak's articles can be read in many popular Catholic magazines. A sought-after speaker on marriage, parenting, and women's spirituality, she has addressed audiences across North America as well as in Australia and Hong Kong.

Founded in 1865, Ave Maria Press,
a ministry of the Congregation of
Holy Cross, is a Catholic publishing
company that serves the spiritual and
formative needs of the Church and its
schools, institutions, and ministers;
Christian individuals and families; and
others seeking spiritual nourishment.

For a complete listing of titles from

Ave Maria Press

Sorin Books

Forest of Peace

Christian Classics

visit www.avemariapress.com

AVE MARIA PRESS
Notre Dame, IN
A Ministry of the United States Province of Holy Cross